THE Wendy PROJECT

Written and Created by
Melissa Jane Osborne

Art, Colors, and Letters by
Veronica Fish

SUPER GENIUS

New York

THE Wendy PROJECT

Written and Created by
Melissa Jane Osborne

Art, Colors, and Letters by
Veronica Fish

Cover by
Veronica Fish

Original Publisher
Maytal Gilboa

Original Graphic Designer
Carla Burgos

Special Thanks
Maria Llorens

EMETCOMICS

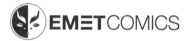

Dawn Guzzo – Production/Design
Melissa Kleynowski – Editorial Intern
Jeff Whitman – Assistant Managing Editor
Jim Salicrup
Editor-in-Chief

PB ISBN: 978-1-62991-769-6
HC ISBN: 978-1-54580-527-5

Super Genius books may be purchased for business or promotional use. For information on bulk purchases please contact Macmillan Corporate and Premium Sales Department at (800) 221-7945 x5442

Super Genius is an imprint of Papercutz

Printed in China, July 2017

Distributed by Macmillan
First Super Genius Printing

SUPER GENIUS

This book belongs to:

Wendy

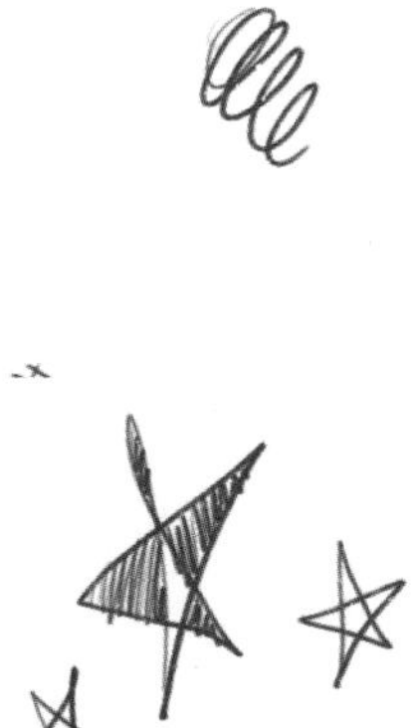

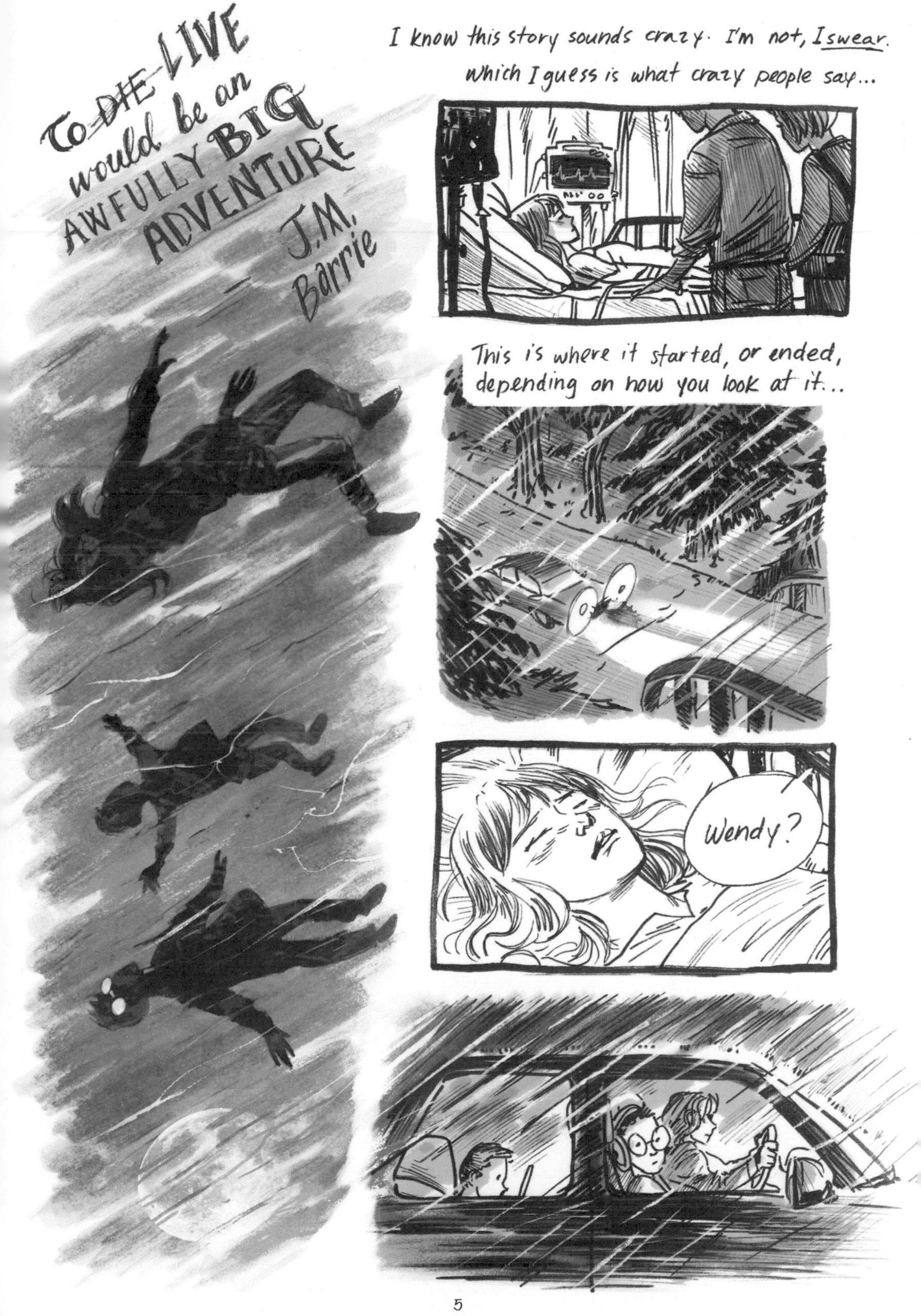
To ~~DIE~~ LIVE
would be an
AWFULLY BIG
ADVENTURE
J.M.
Barrie
I know this story sounds crazy. I'm not, I swear.
which I guess is what crazy people say...
This is where it started, or ended,
depending on how you look at it...
Wendy?

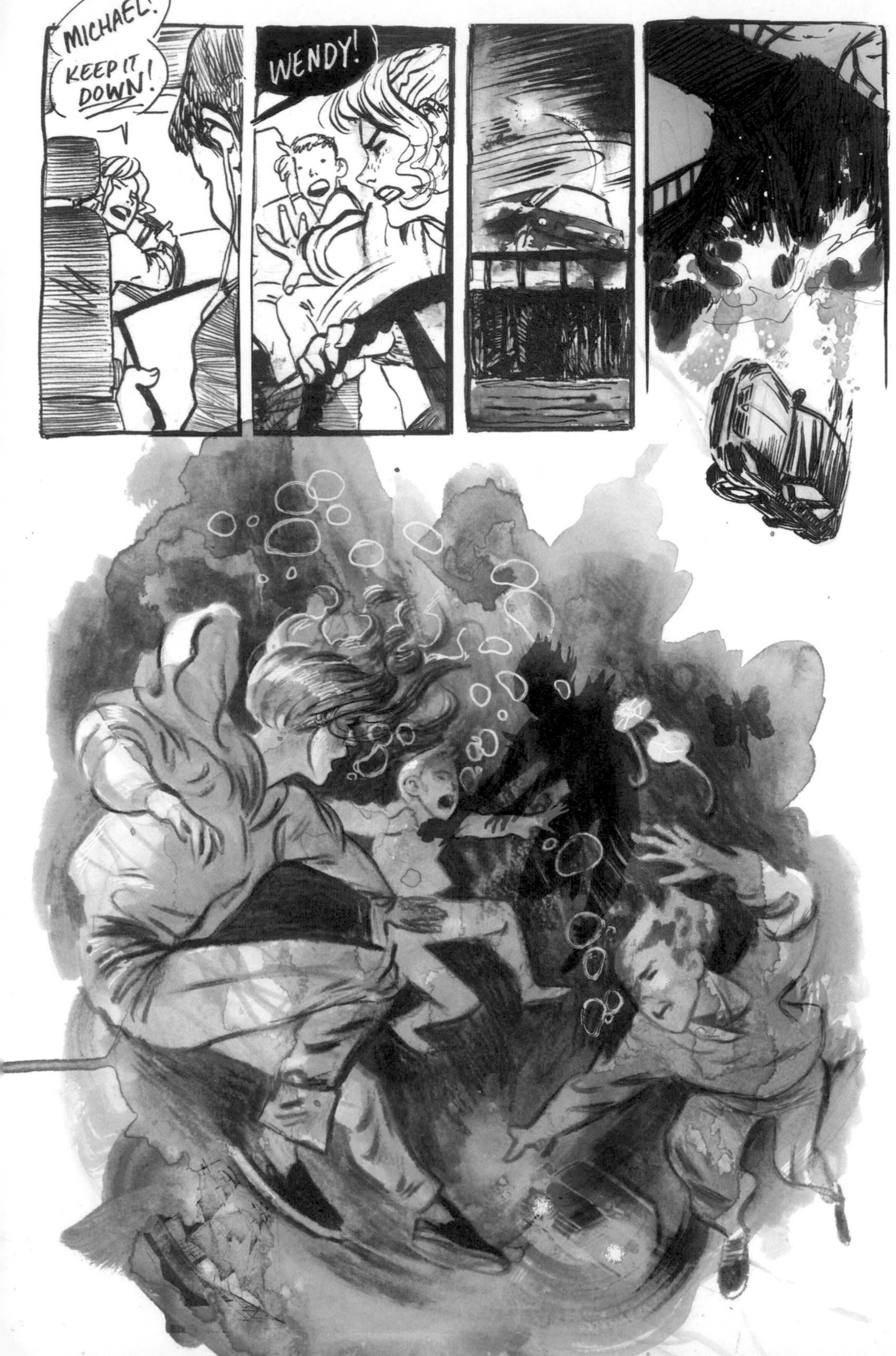
MICHAEL!
KEEP IT DOWN!
WENDY!

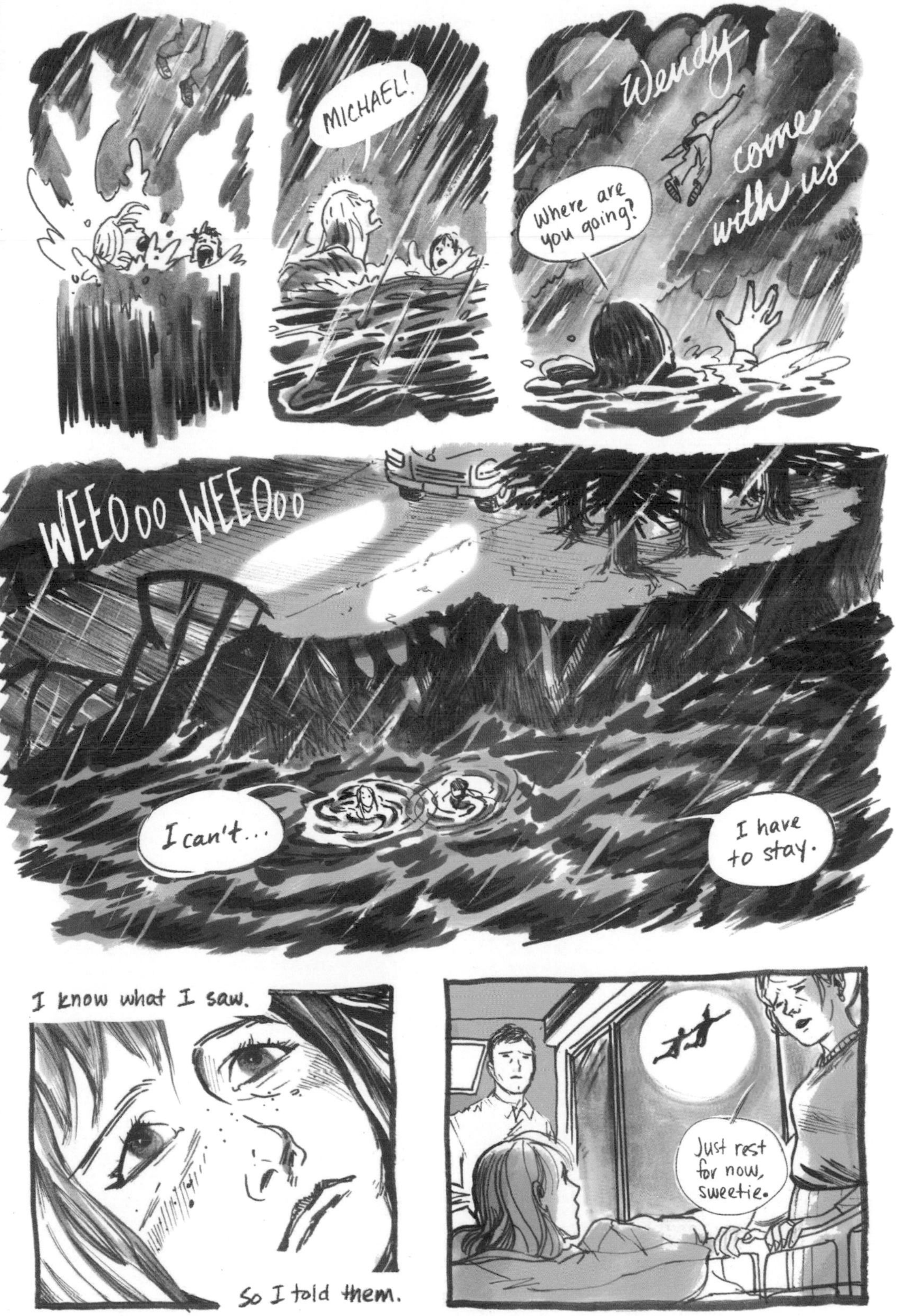
MICHAEL!
Wendy
come with us
Where are you going?
WEEOoo WEEOoo
I can't...
I have to stay.
I know what I saw.
So I told them.
Just rest for now, sweetie.

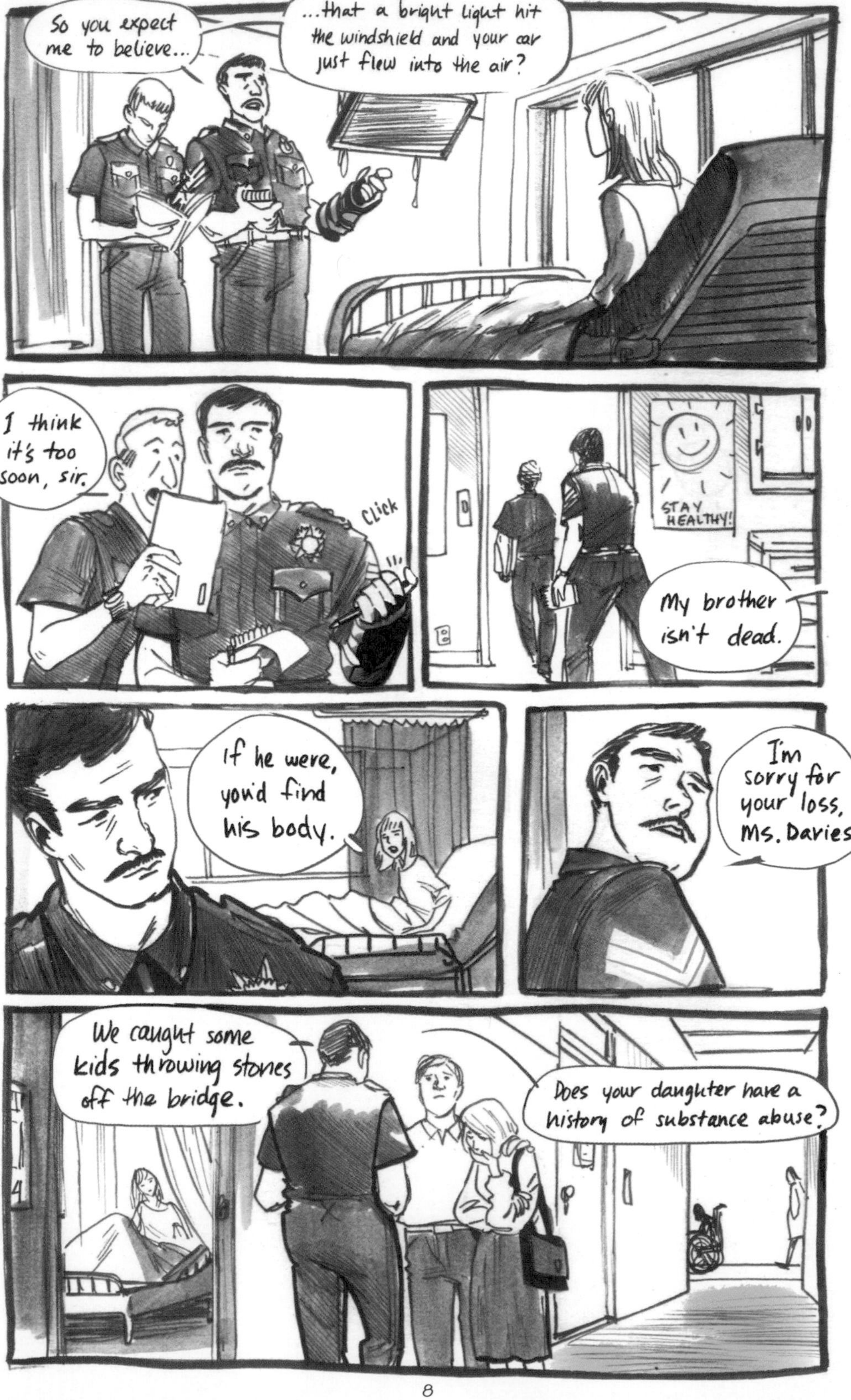

So you expect me to believe...
...that a bright light hit the windshield and your car just flew into the air?
I think it's too soon, sir.
Click
STAY HEALTHY!
My brother isn't dead.
If he were, you'd find his body.
I'm sorry for your loss, Ms. Davies
We caught some kids throwing stones off the bridge.
Does your daughter have a history of substance abuse?

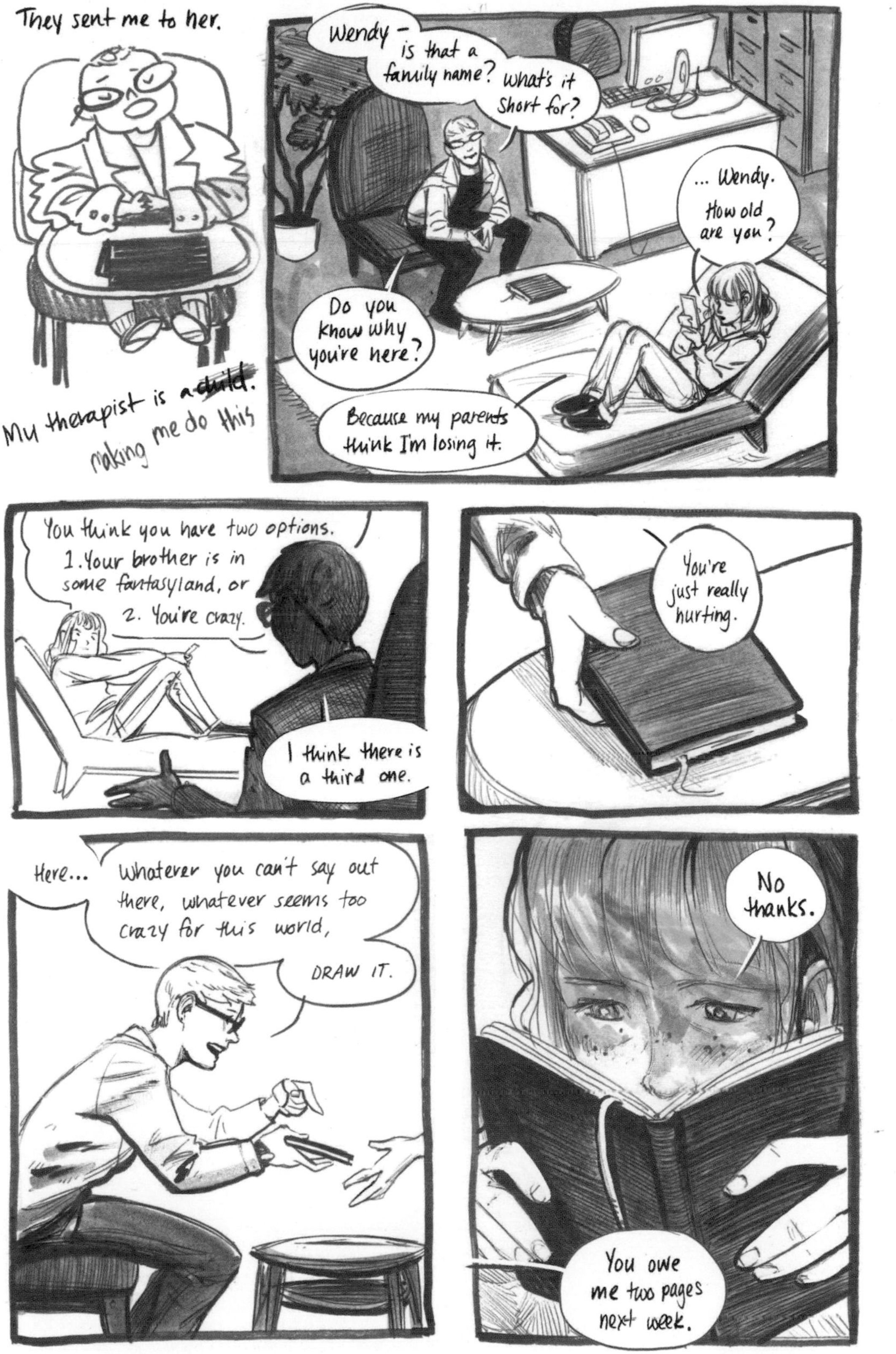

They sent me to her.
My therapist is ~~a child~~.
making me do this
Wendy – is that a family name?
what's it short for?
... Wendy.
How old are you?
Do you know why you're here?
Because my parents think I'm losing it.
You think you have two options. 1. Your brother is in some fantasyland, or 2. You're crazy.
I think there is a third one.
You're just really hurting.
Here...
Whatever you can't say out there, whatever seems too crazy for this world,
DRAW IT.
No thanks.
You owe me two pages next week.

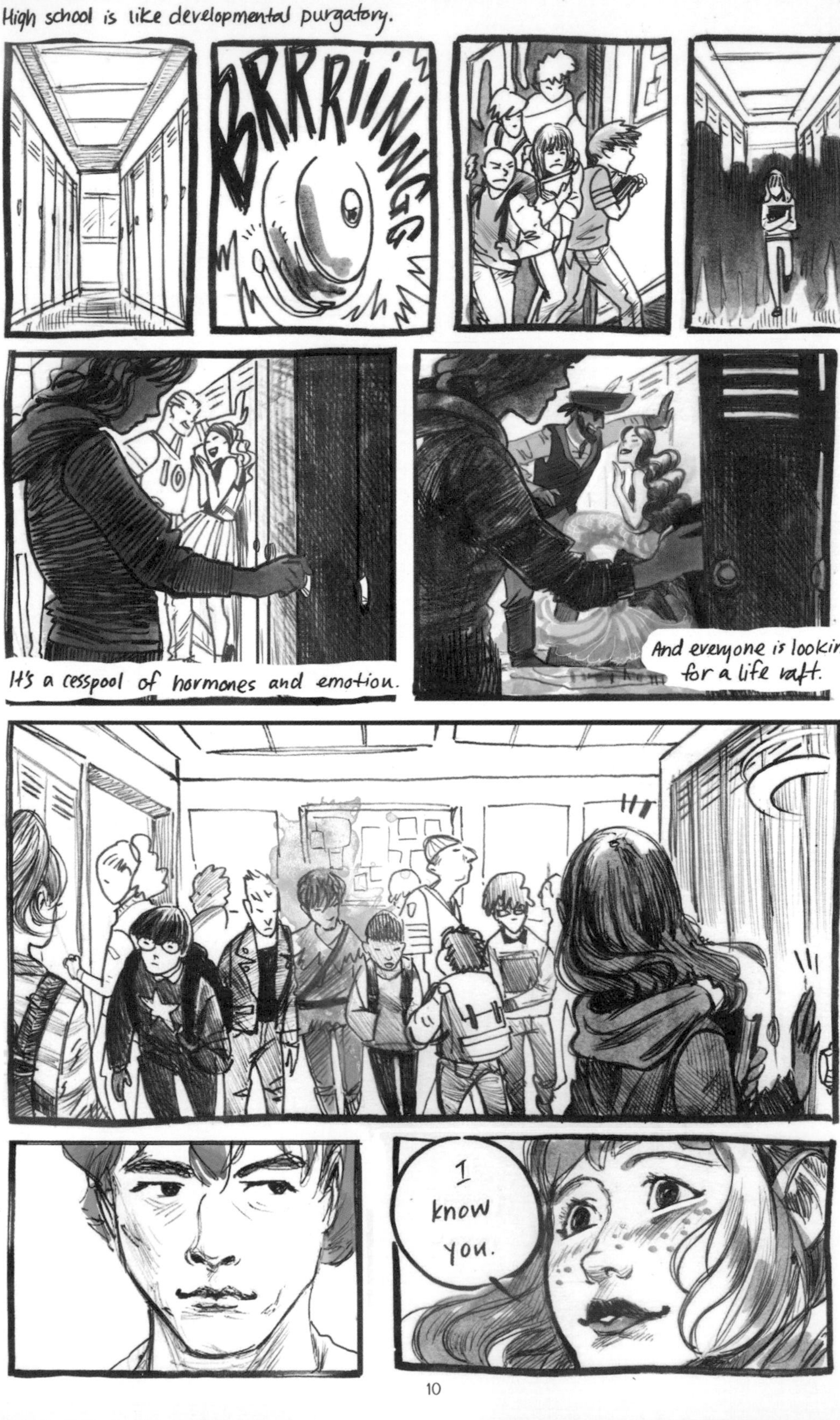
High school is like developmental purgatory.
BRRRIINNGG
It's a cesspool of hormones and emotion.
And everyone is looking for a life raft.
I know you.

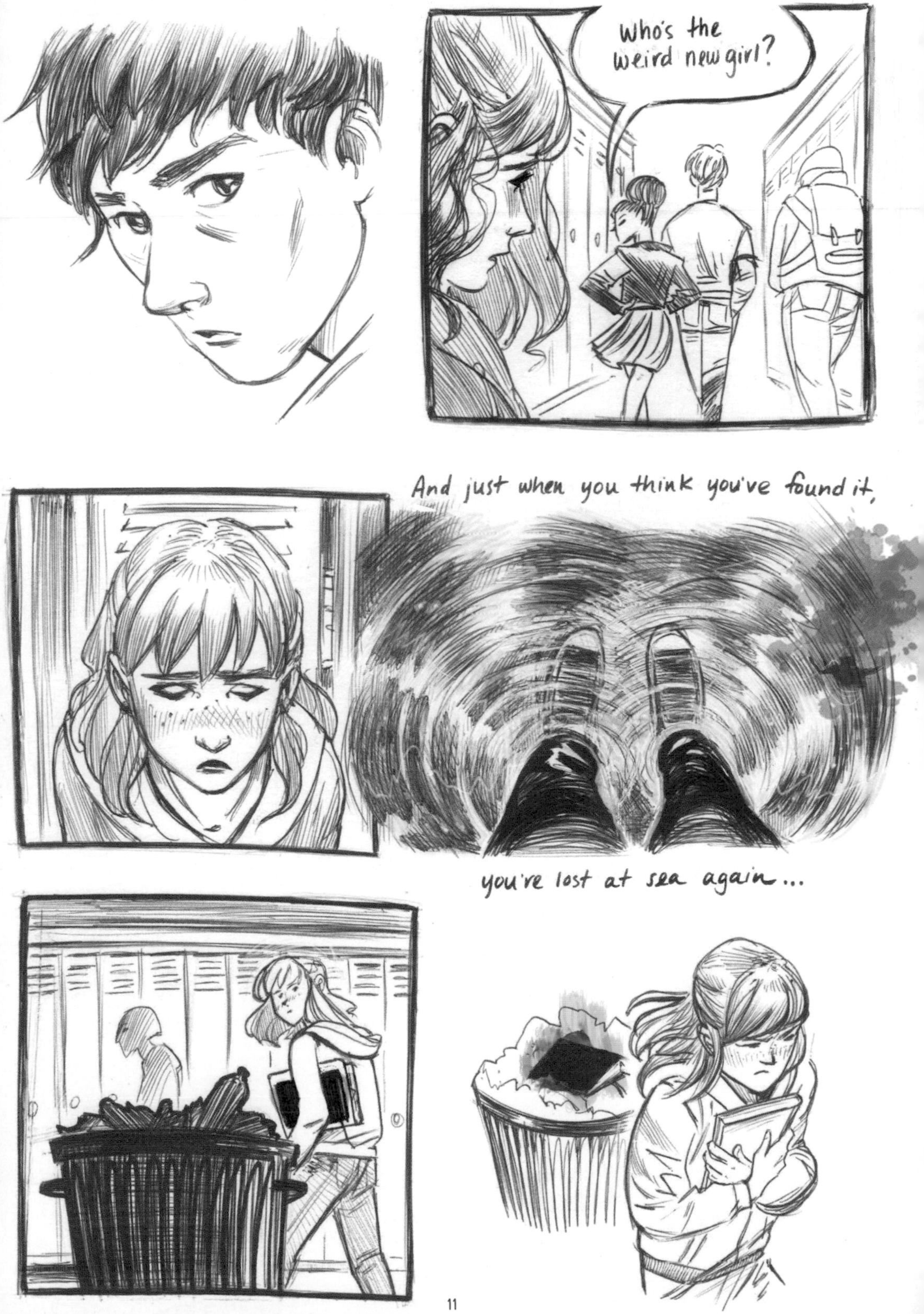
Who's the weird new girl?
And just when you think you've found it,
you're lost at sea again...

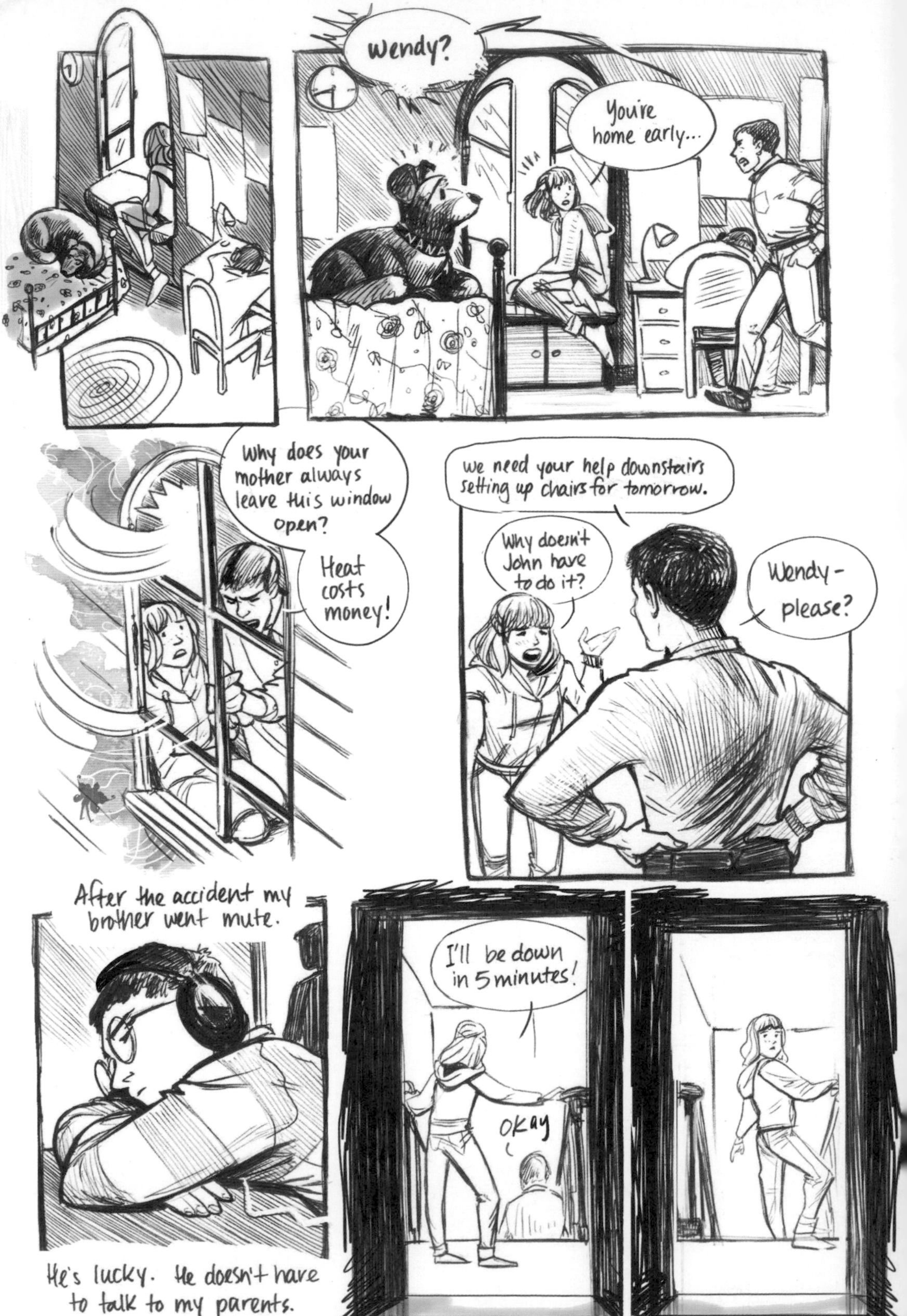

Wendy?
You're home early...
NANA
Why does your mother always leave this window open?
Heat costs money!
we need your help downstairs setting up chairs for tomorrow.
Why doesn't John have to do it?
Wendy - please?
After the accident my brother went mute.
He's lucky. He doesn't have to talk to my parents.
I'll be down in 5 minutes!
OKay

John is sharing my room for now.
We decided not to touch the boys' room.

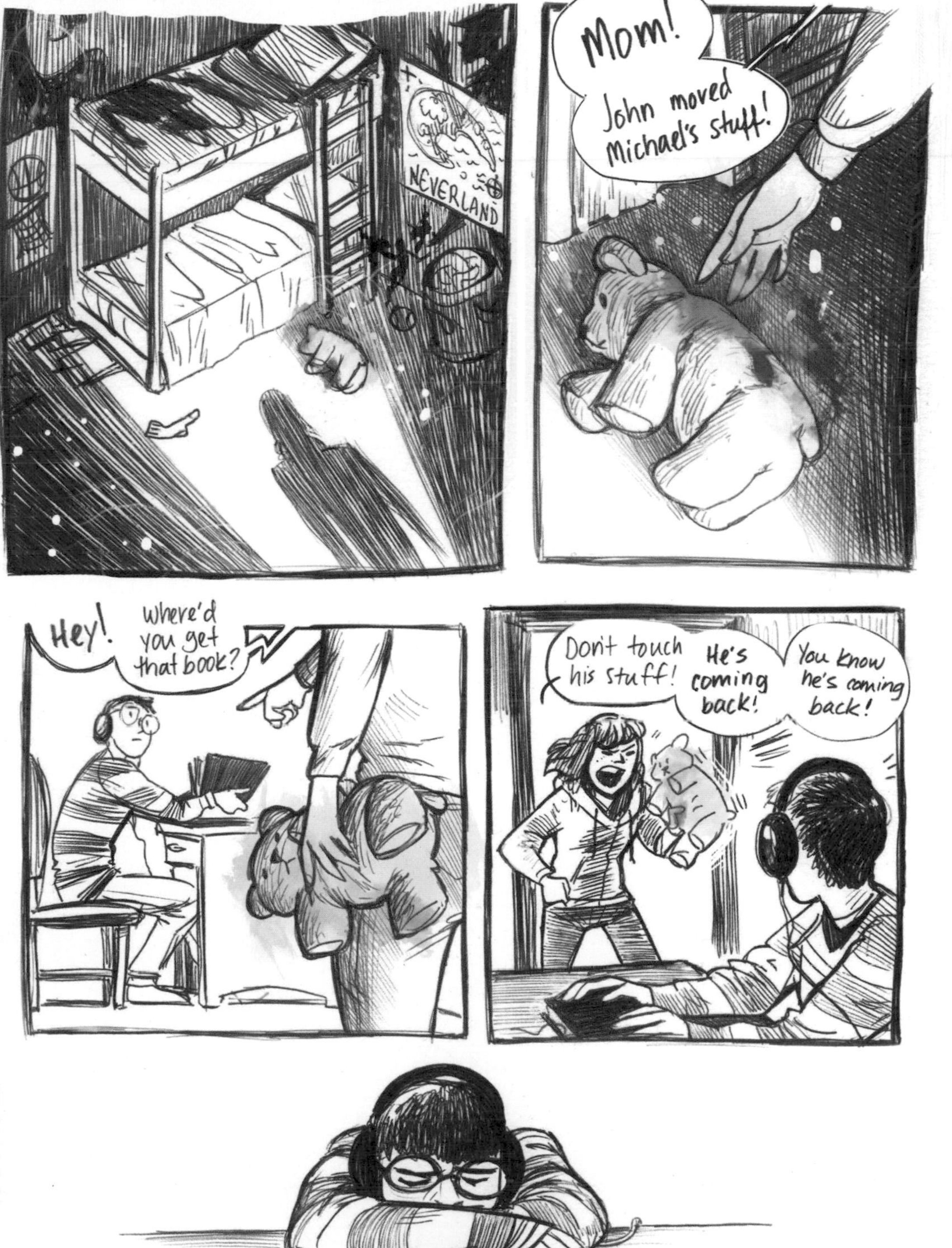
NEVERLAND
Mom!
John moved Michael's stuff!
Hey!
Where'd you get that book?
Don't touch his stuff!
He's coming back!
You know he's coming back!

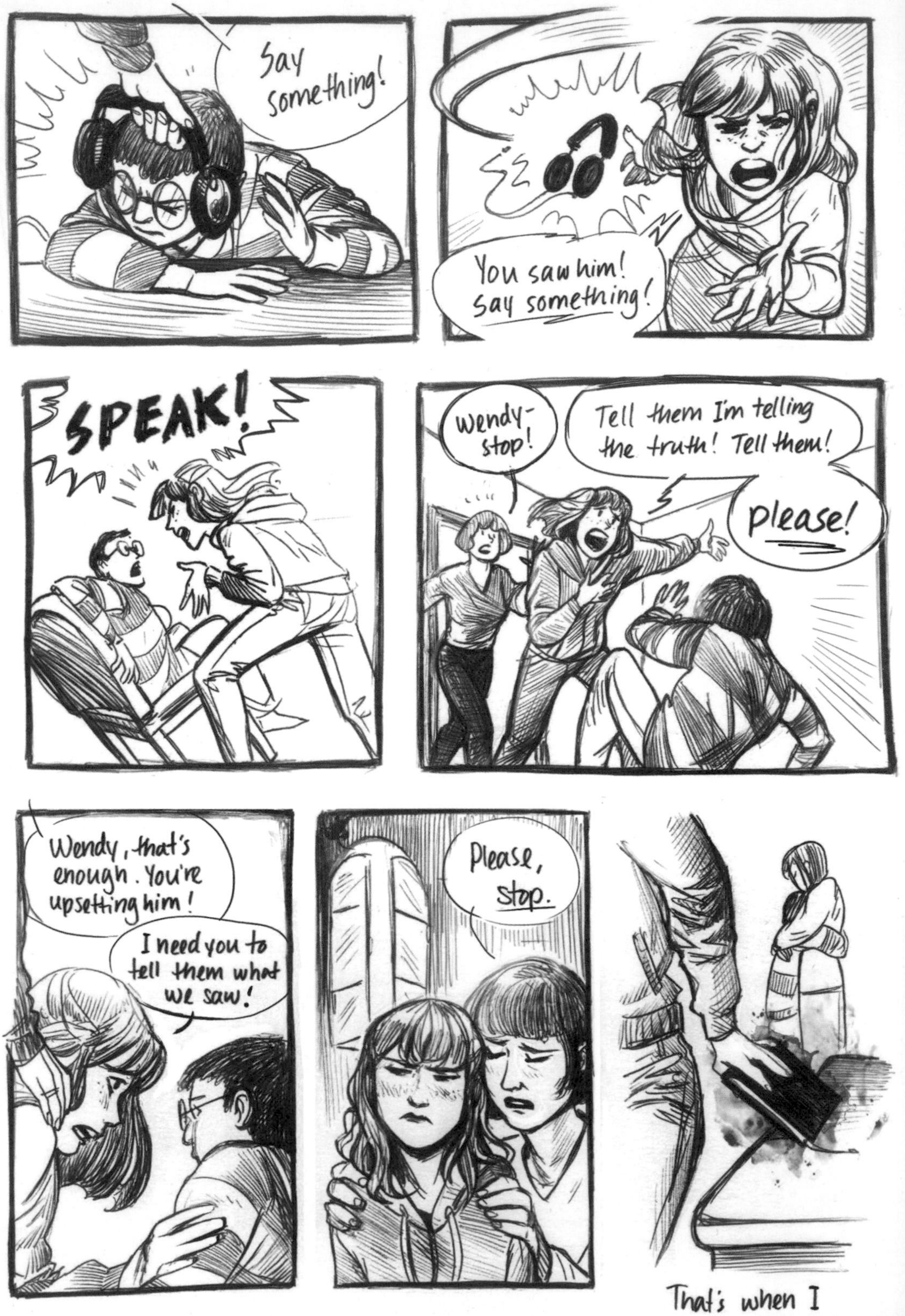
Say something!
You saw him! Say something!
SPEAK!
Wendy-stop!
Tell them I'm telling the truth! Tell them!
please!
Wendy, that's enough. You're upsetting him!
I need you to tell them what we saw!
Please, stop.
That's when I started drawing.

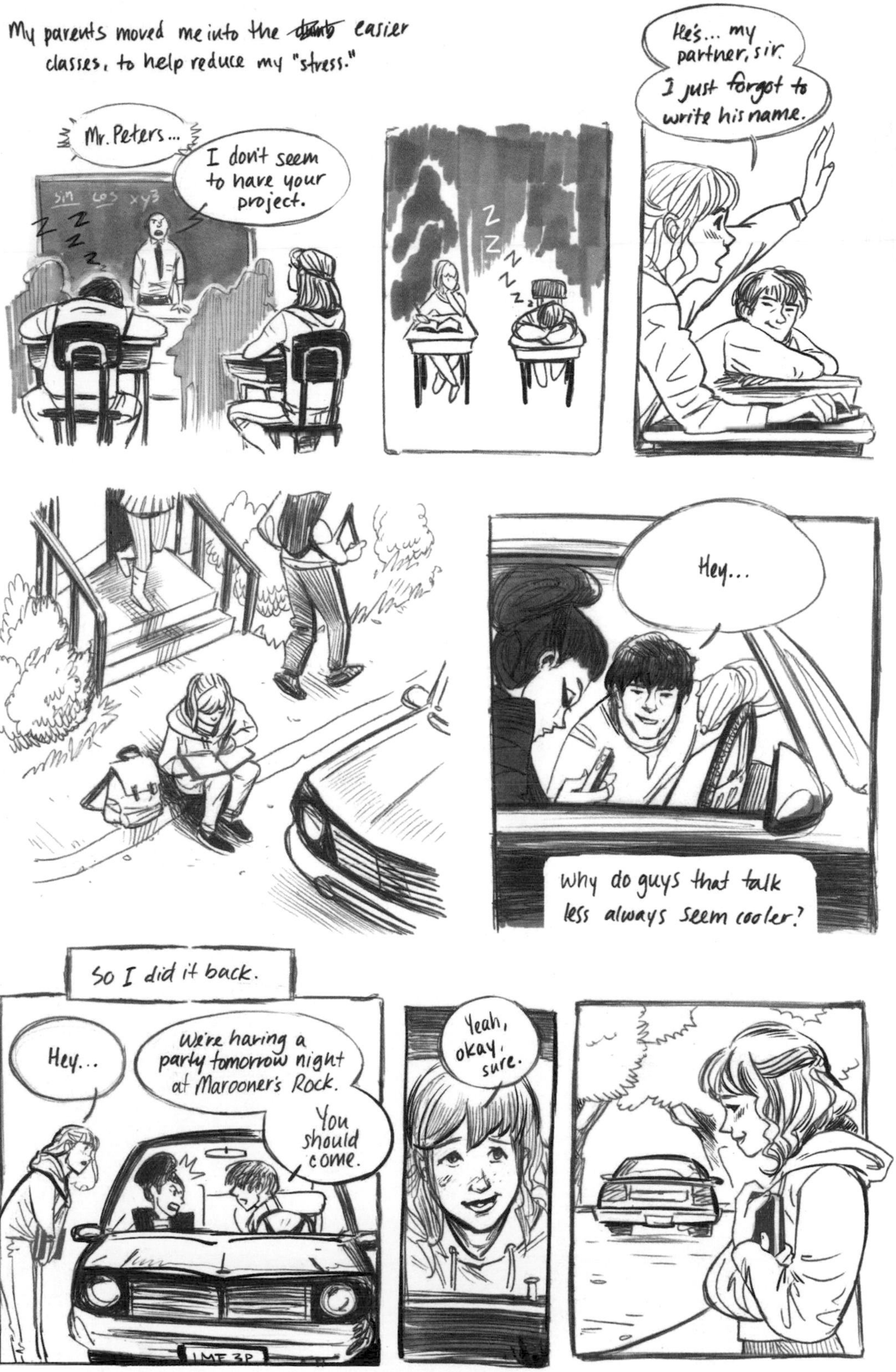

My parents moved me into the easier classes, to help reduce my "stress."
Mr. Peters...
I don't seem to have your project.
He's... my partner, sir.
I just forgot to write his name.
Hey...
Why do guys that talk less always seem cooler?
So I did it back.
Hey...
We're having a party tomorrow night at Marooner's Rock.
You should come.
Yeah, okay, sure.

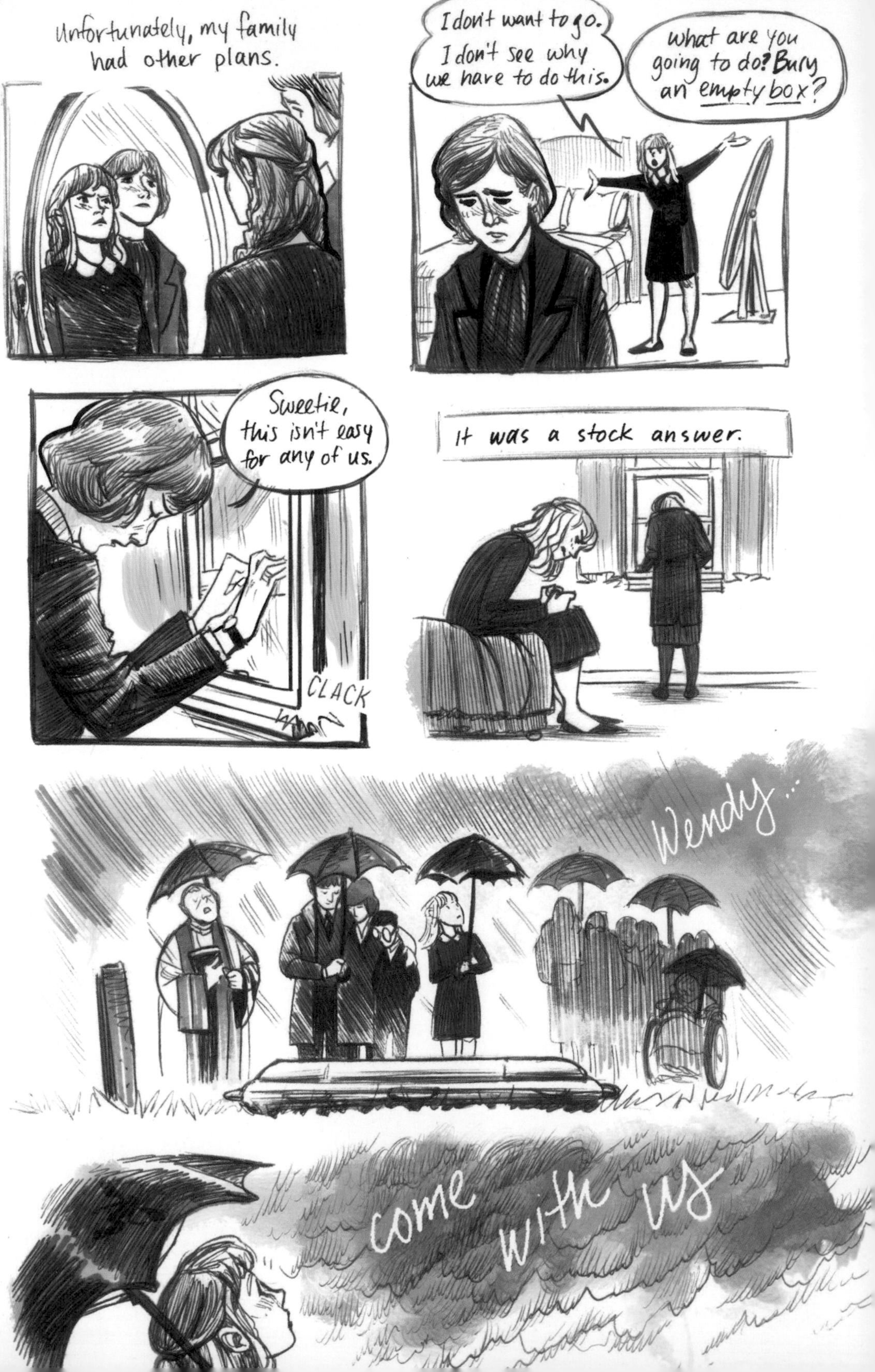
Unfortunately, my family had other plans.
I don't want to go. I don't see why we have to do this.
What are you going to do? Bury an empty box?
Sweetie, this isn't easy for any of us.
CLACK
It was a stock answer.
Wendy...
come with us

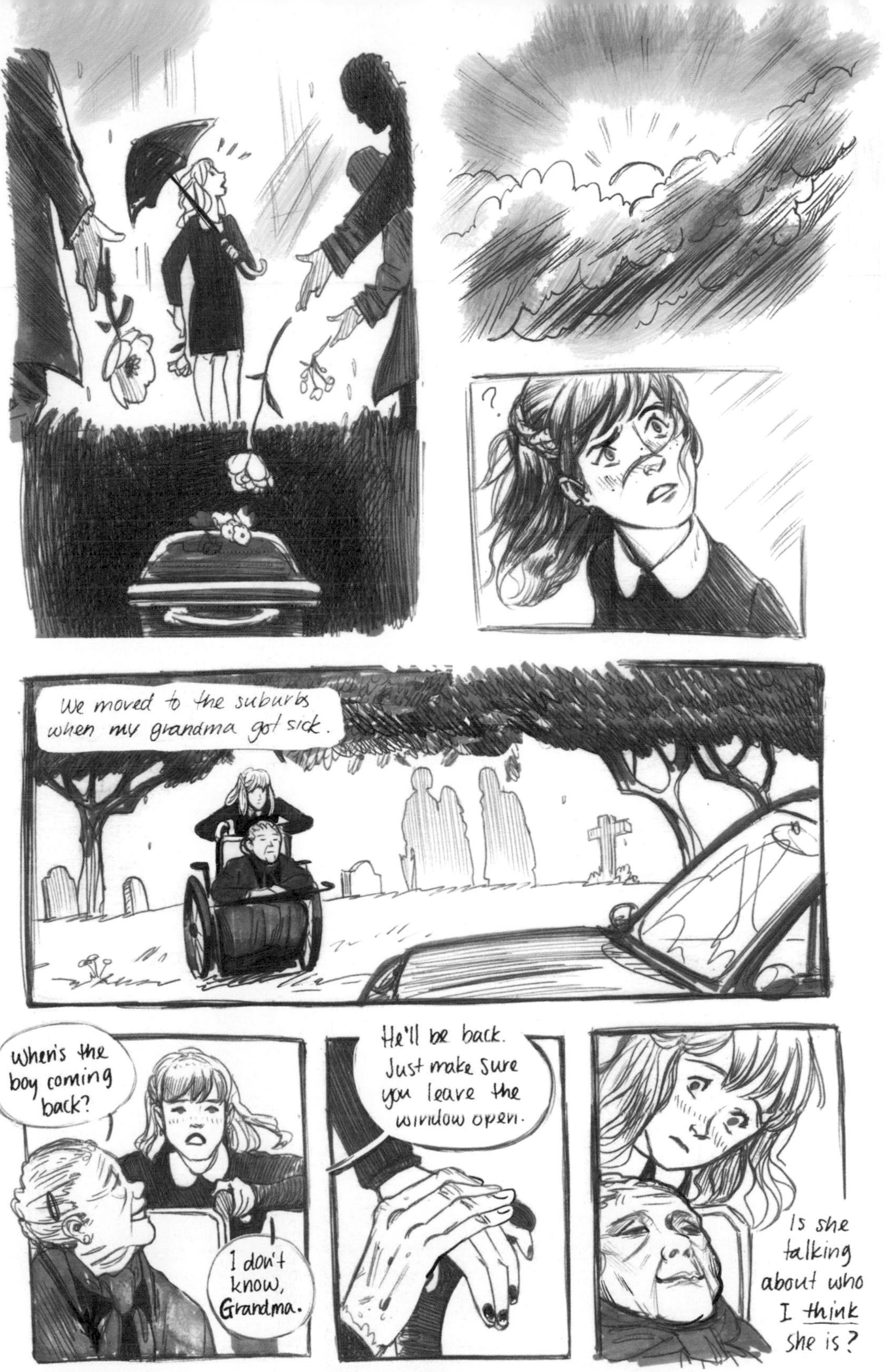

?
We moved to the suburbs when my grandma got sick.
When's the boy coming back?
I don't know, Grandma.
He'll be back. Just make sure you leave the window open.
Is she talking about who I think she is?

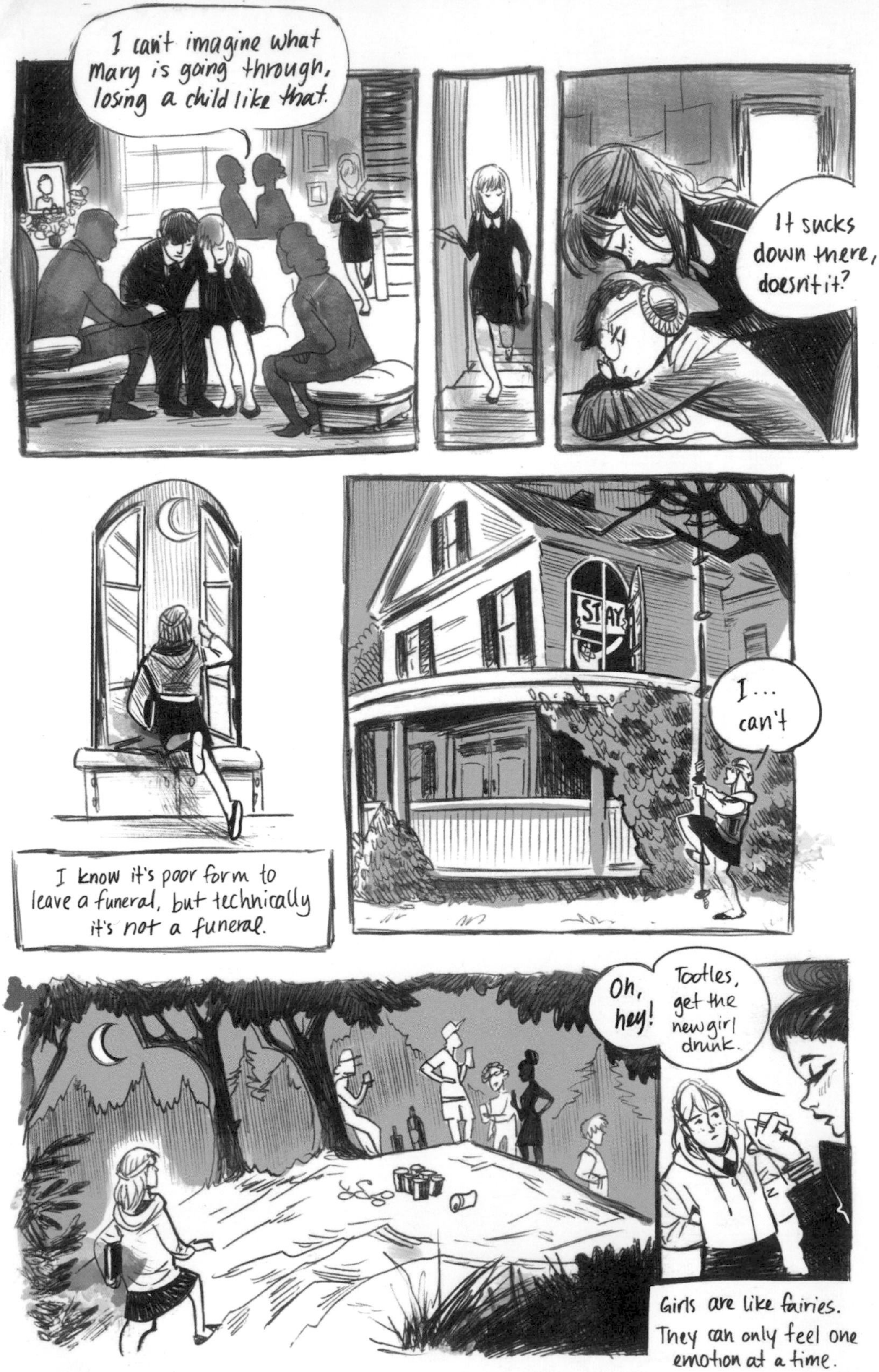
I can't imagine what mary is going through, losing a child like that.
It sucks down there, doesn't it?
I know it's poor form to leave a funeral, but technically it's not a funeral.
STAY
I... can't
Oh, hey!
Tootles, get the new girl drunk.
Girls are like fairies. They can only feel one emotion at a time.

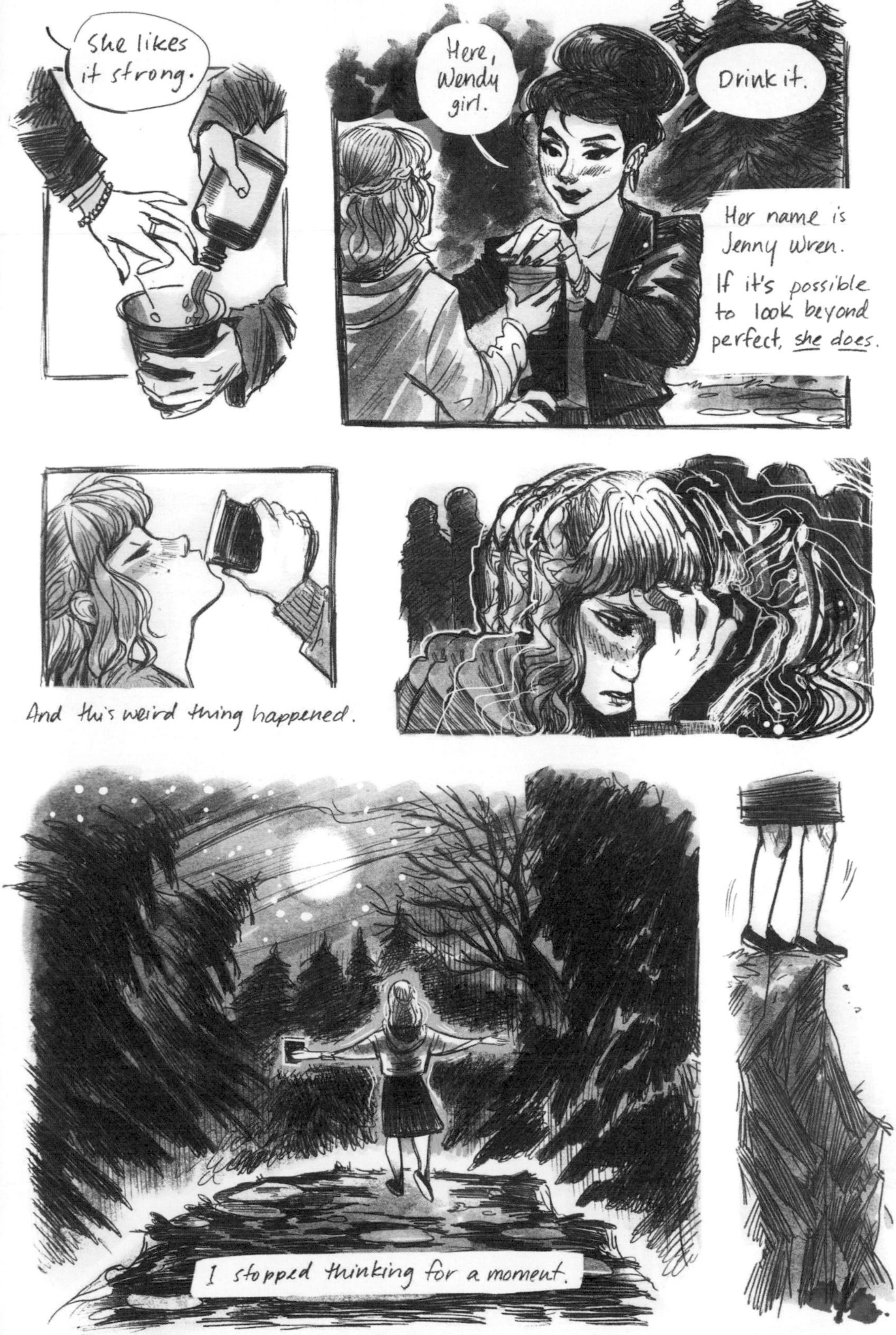

She likes it strong.
Here, Wendy girl.
Drink it.
Her name is Jenny Wren. If it's possible to look beyond perfect, she does.
And this weird thing happened.
I stopped thinking for a moment.

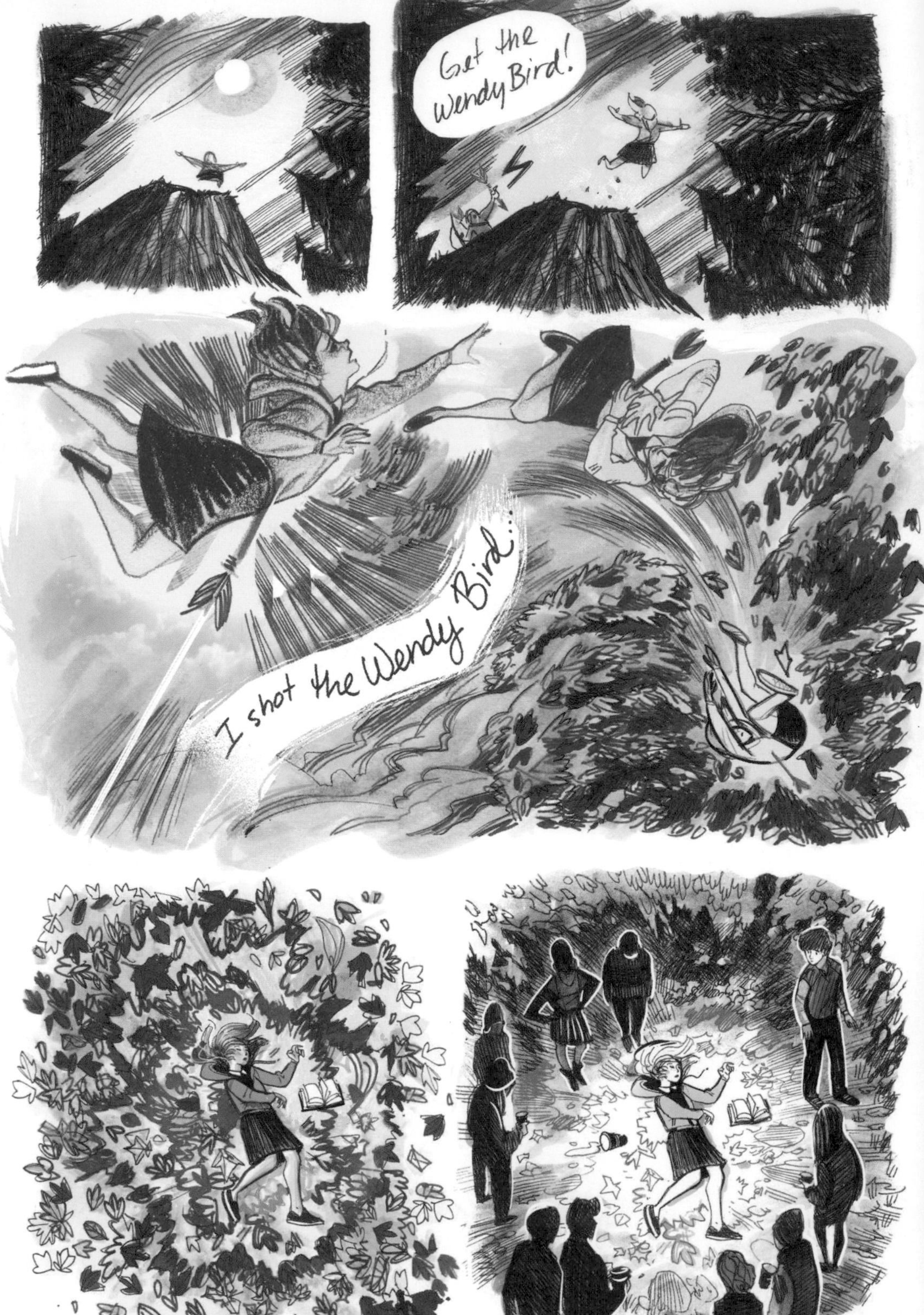
Get the Wendy Bird!
I shot the Wendy Bird...

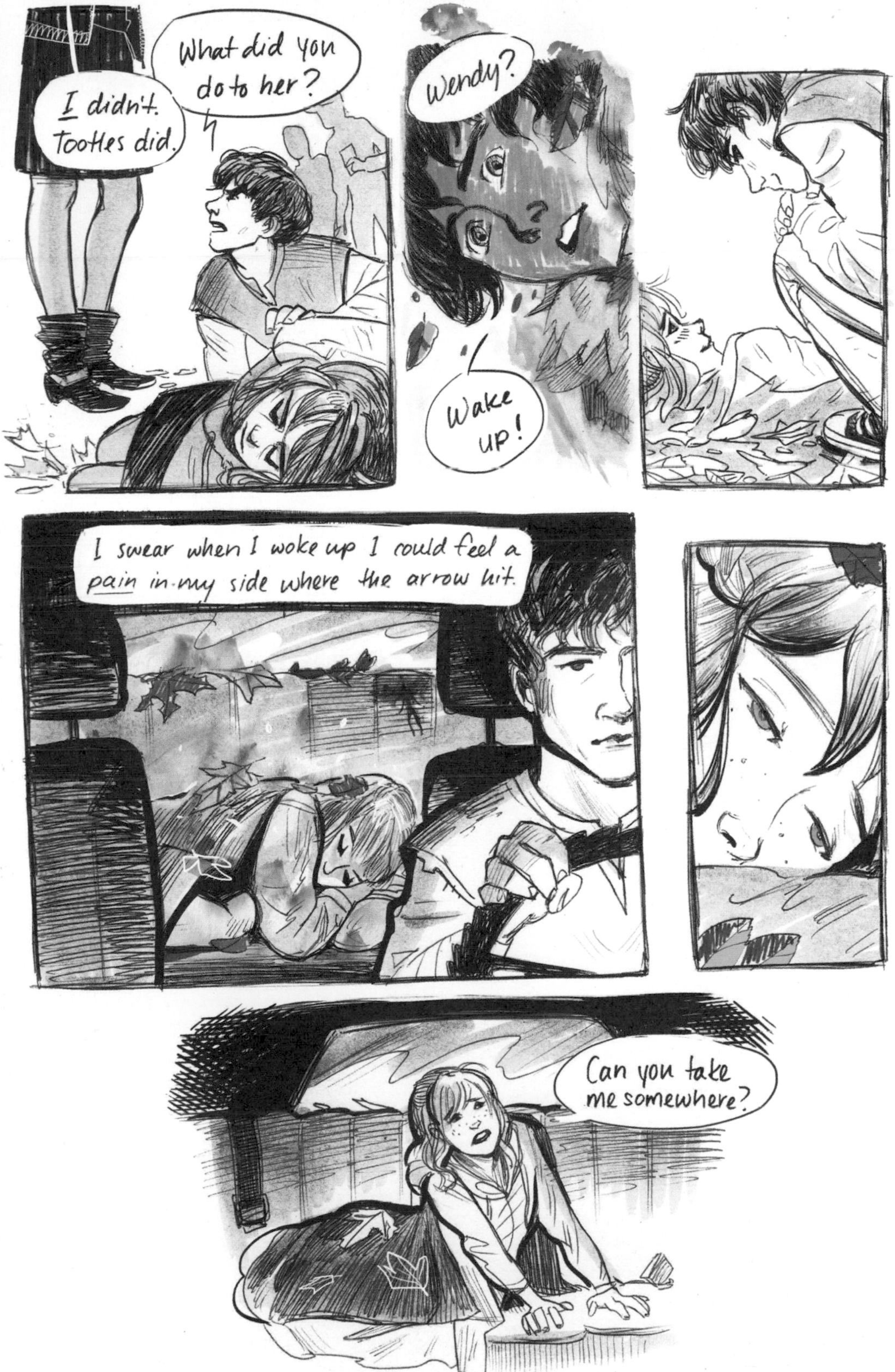
What did you do to her?
I didn't. Tootles did.
Wendy?
Wake up!
I swear when I woke up I could feel a pain in my side where the arrow hit.
Can you take me somewhere?

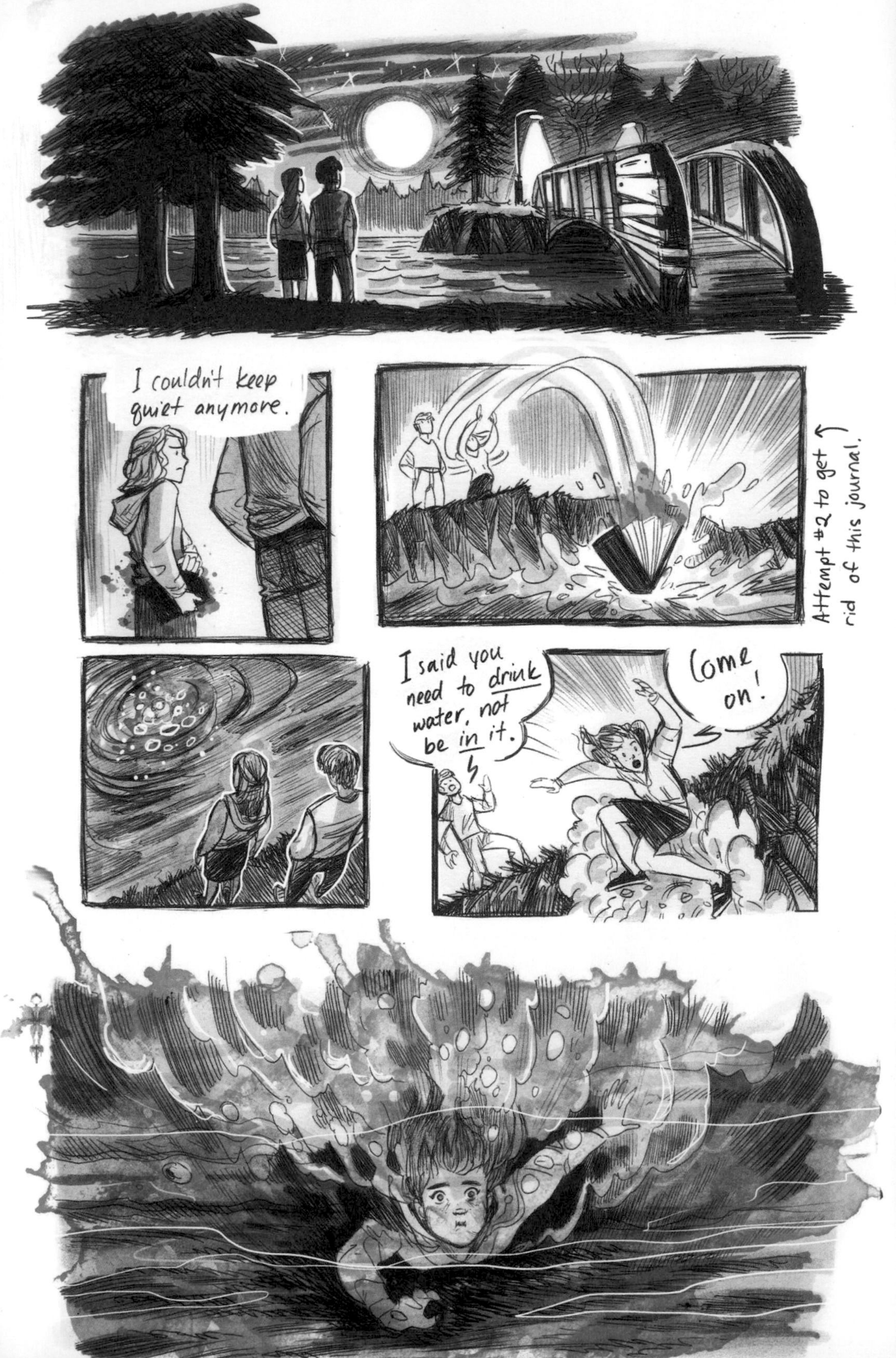
I couldn't keep quiet anymore.
Attempt #2 to get rid of this journal.
I said you need to drink water, not be in it.
Come on!

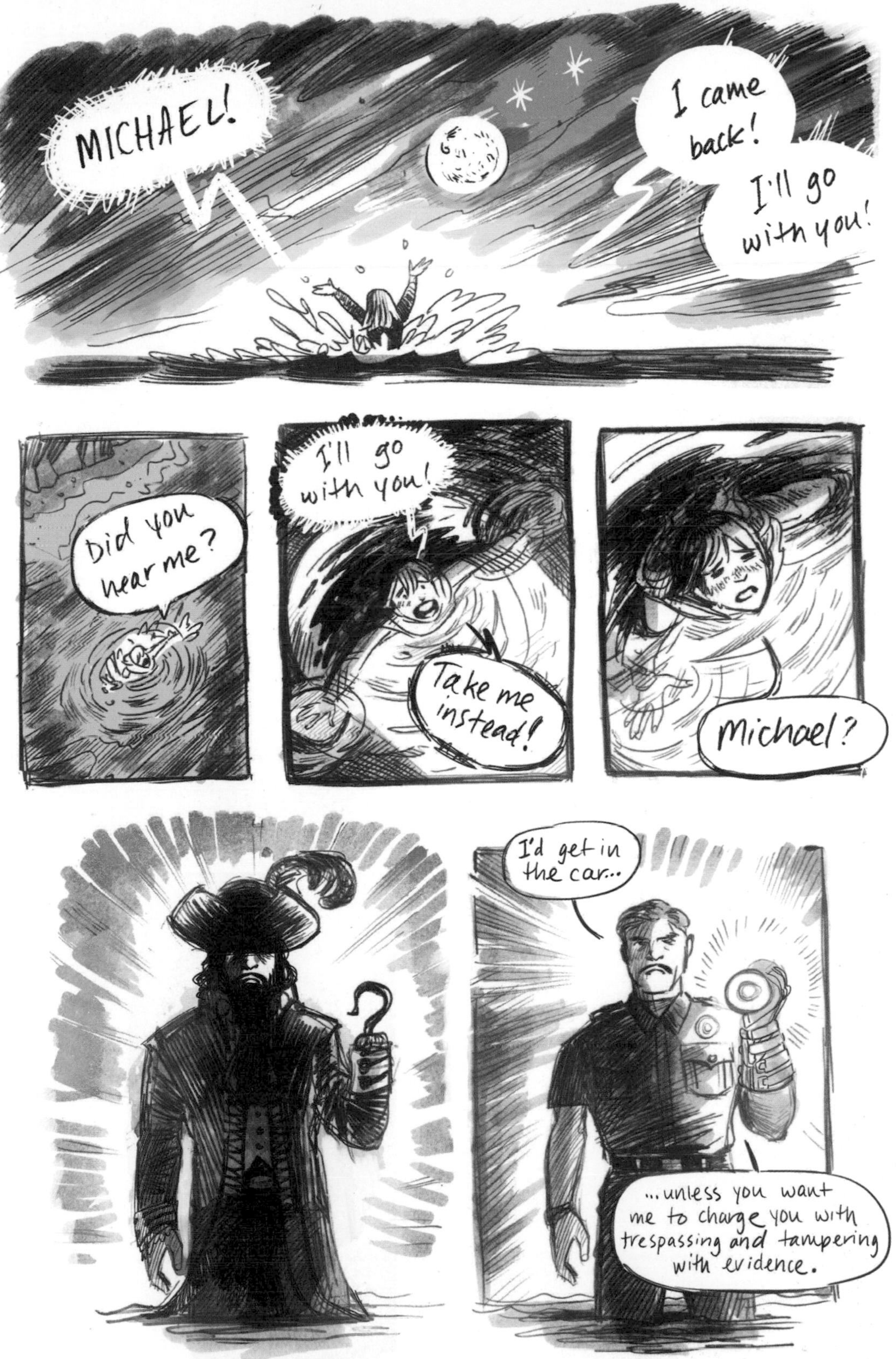
MICHAEL!
I came back!
I'll go with you!
Did you hear me?
I'll go with you!
Take me instead!
Michael?
I'd get in the car...
...unless you want me to charge you with trespassing and tampering with evidence.

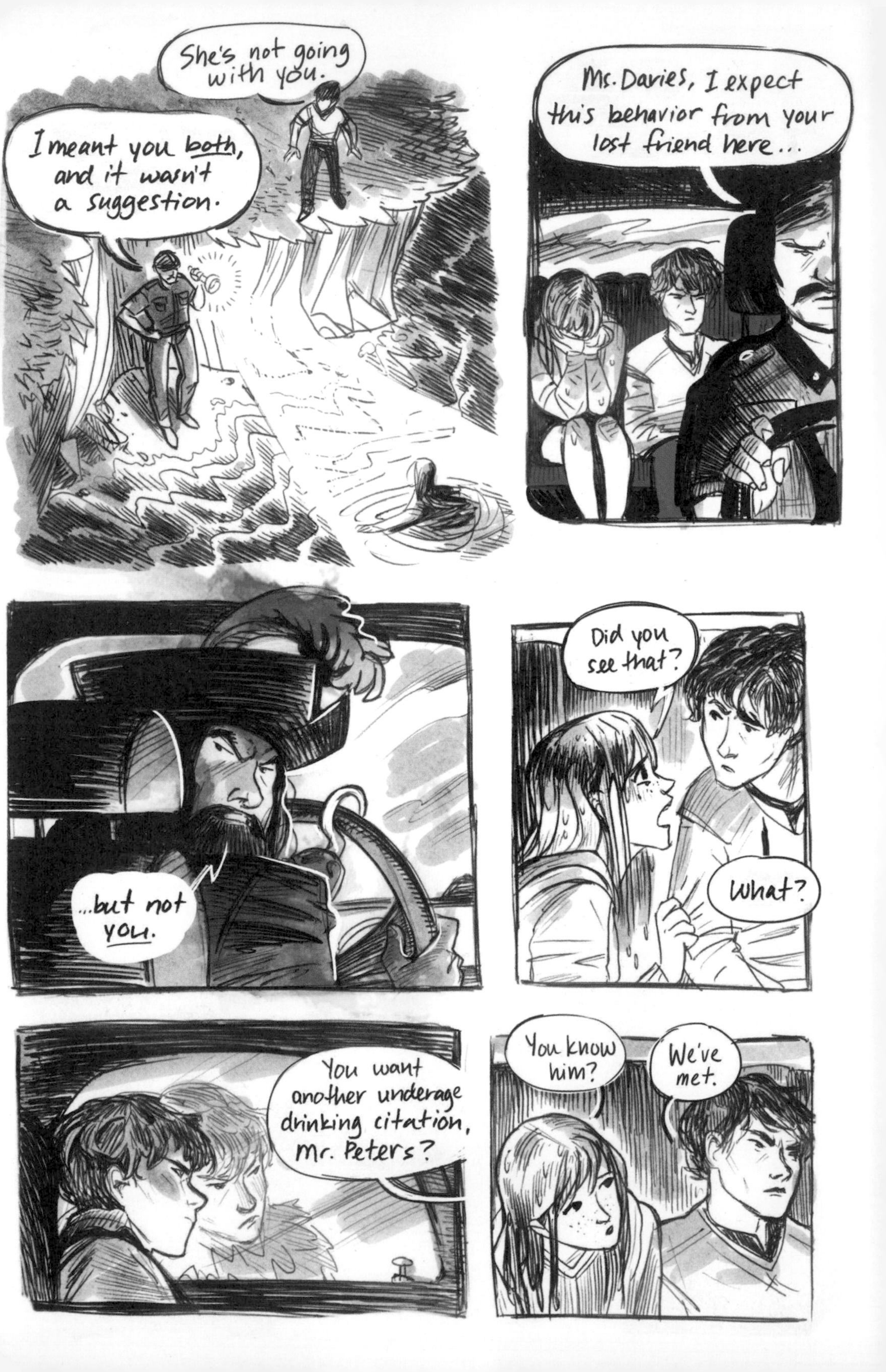
She's not going with you.
I meant you both, and it wasn't a suggestion.
Ms. Davies, I expect this behavior from your lost friend here...
...but not you.
Did you see that?
What?
You want another underage drinking citation, Mr. Peters?
You know him?
We've met.

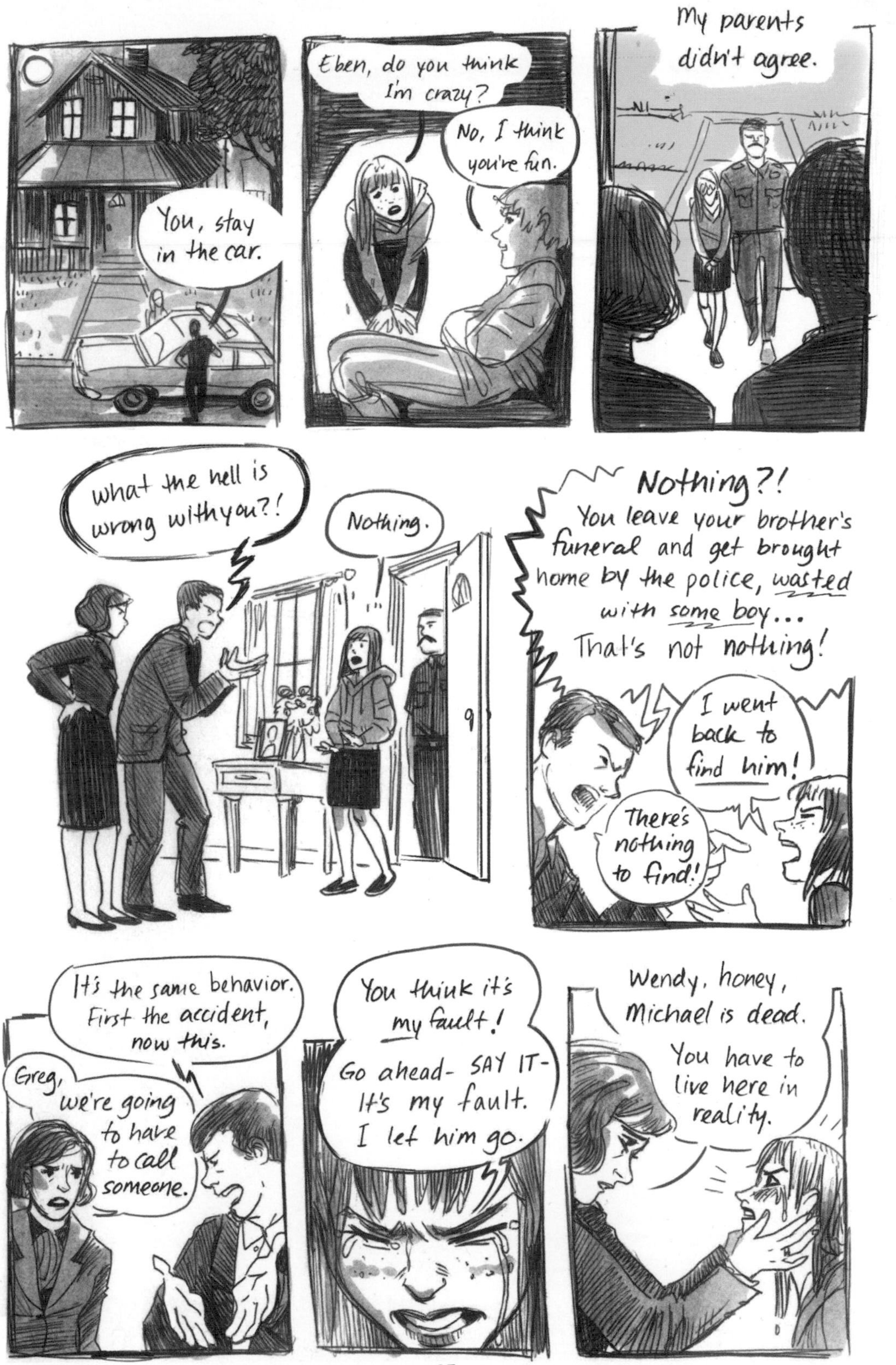
You, stay in the car.
Eben, do you think I'm crazy?
No, I think you're fun.
My parents didn't agree.
what the hell is wrong with you?!
Nothing.
Nothing?! You leave your brother's funeral and get brought home by the police, wasted with some boy... That's not nothing!
I went back to find him!
There's nothing to find!
It's the same behavior. First the accident, now this.
Greg, we're going to have to call someone.
You think it's my fault!
Go ahead- SAY IT- It's my fault. I let him go.
Wendy, honey, Michael is dead.
You have to live here in reality.

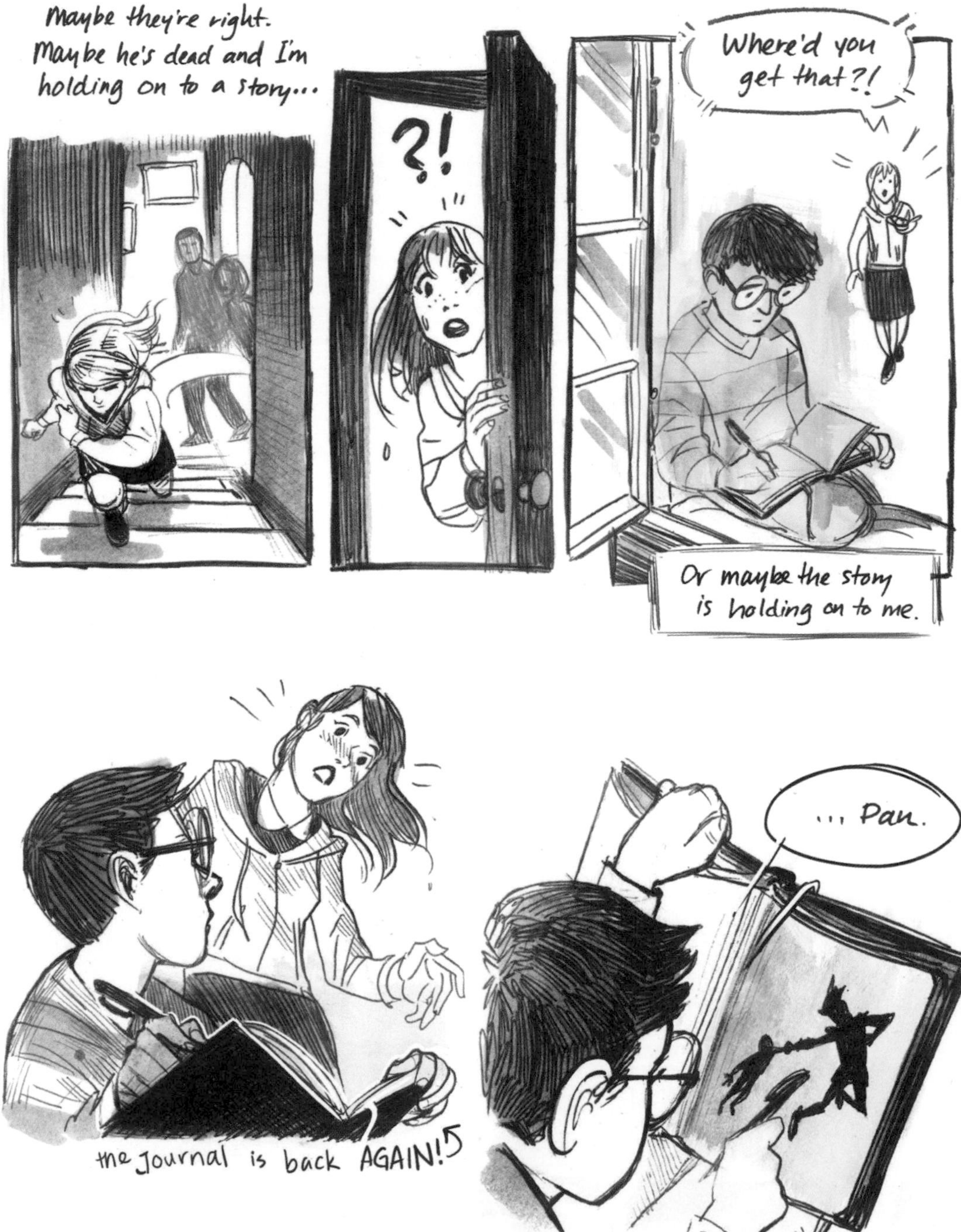
Maybe they're right. Maybe he's dead and I'm holding on to a story...
?!
Where'd you get that?!
Or maybe the story is holding on to me.
the Journal is back AGAIN![5]
... Pan.

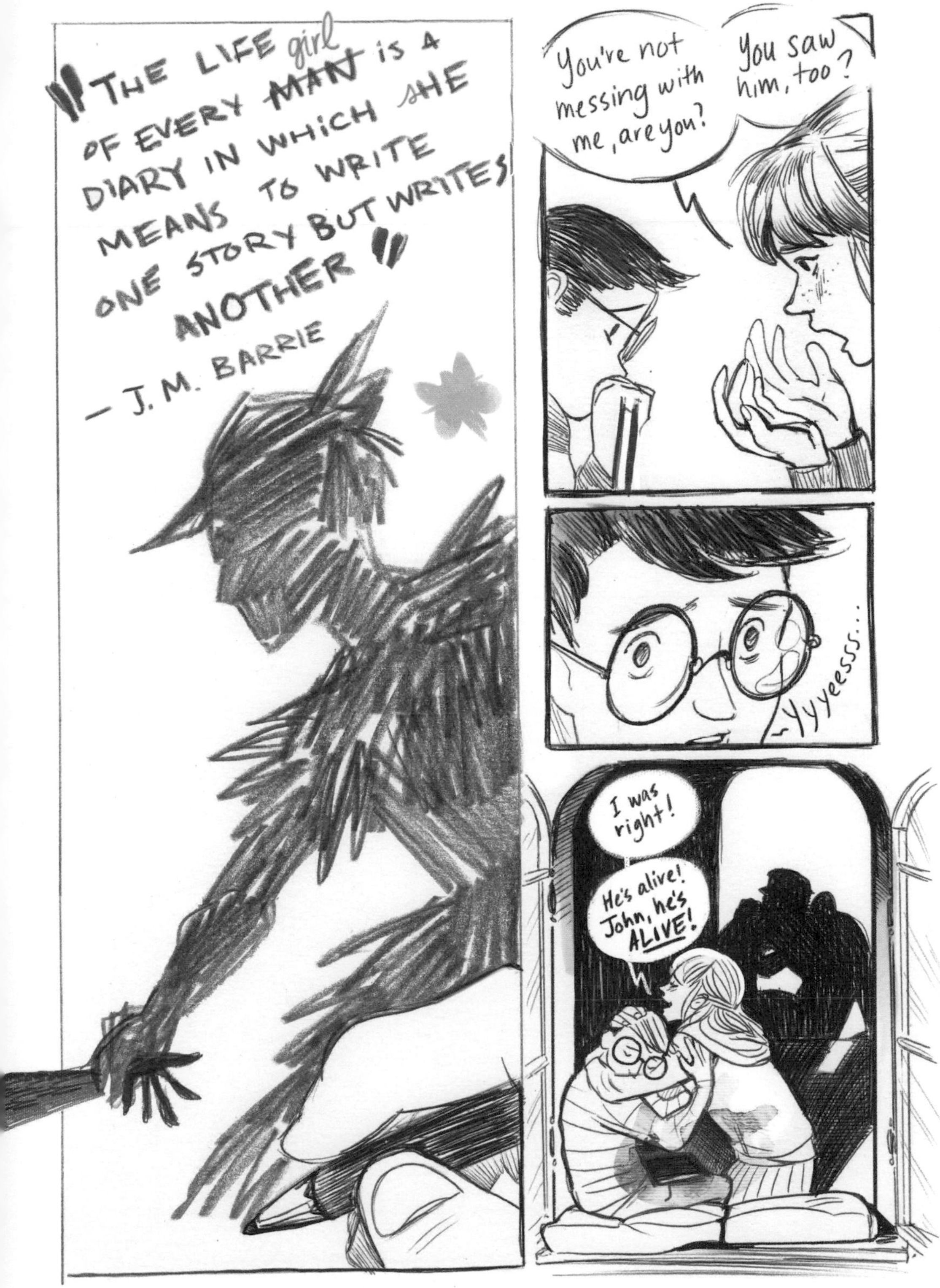

"THE LIFE OF EVERY ~~MAN~~ girl IS A DIARY IN WHICH ~~HE~~ SHE MEANS TO WRITE ONE STORY BUT WRITES ANOTHER"
– J. M. BARRIE
You're not messing with me, are you?
You saw him, too?
Yyyeesss...
I was right!
He's alive! John, he's ALIVE!

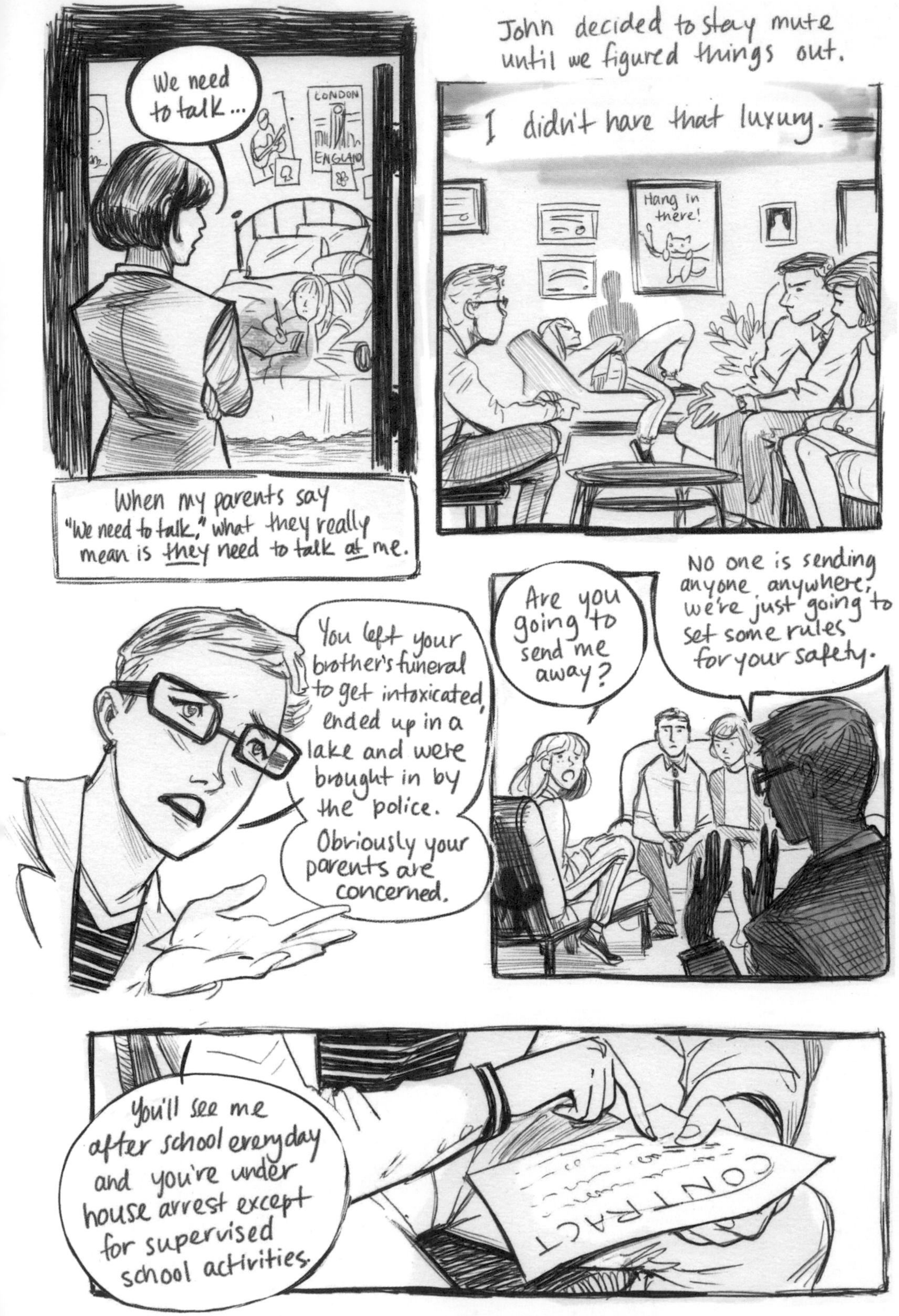

We need to talk...
LONDON
ENGLAND
When my parents say "We need to talk," what they really mean is they need to talk at me.
John decided to stay mute until we figured things out.
I didn't have that luxury.
Hang in there!
You left your brother's funeral to get intoxicated, ended up in a lake and were brought in by the police.
Obviously your parents are concerned.
Are you going to send me away?
No one is sending anyone anywhere, we're just going to set some rules for your safety.
You'll see me after school everyday and you're under house arrest except for supervised school activities.
CONTRACT

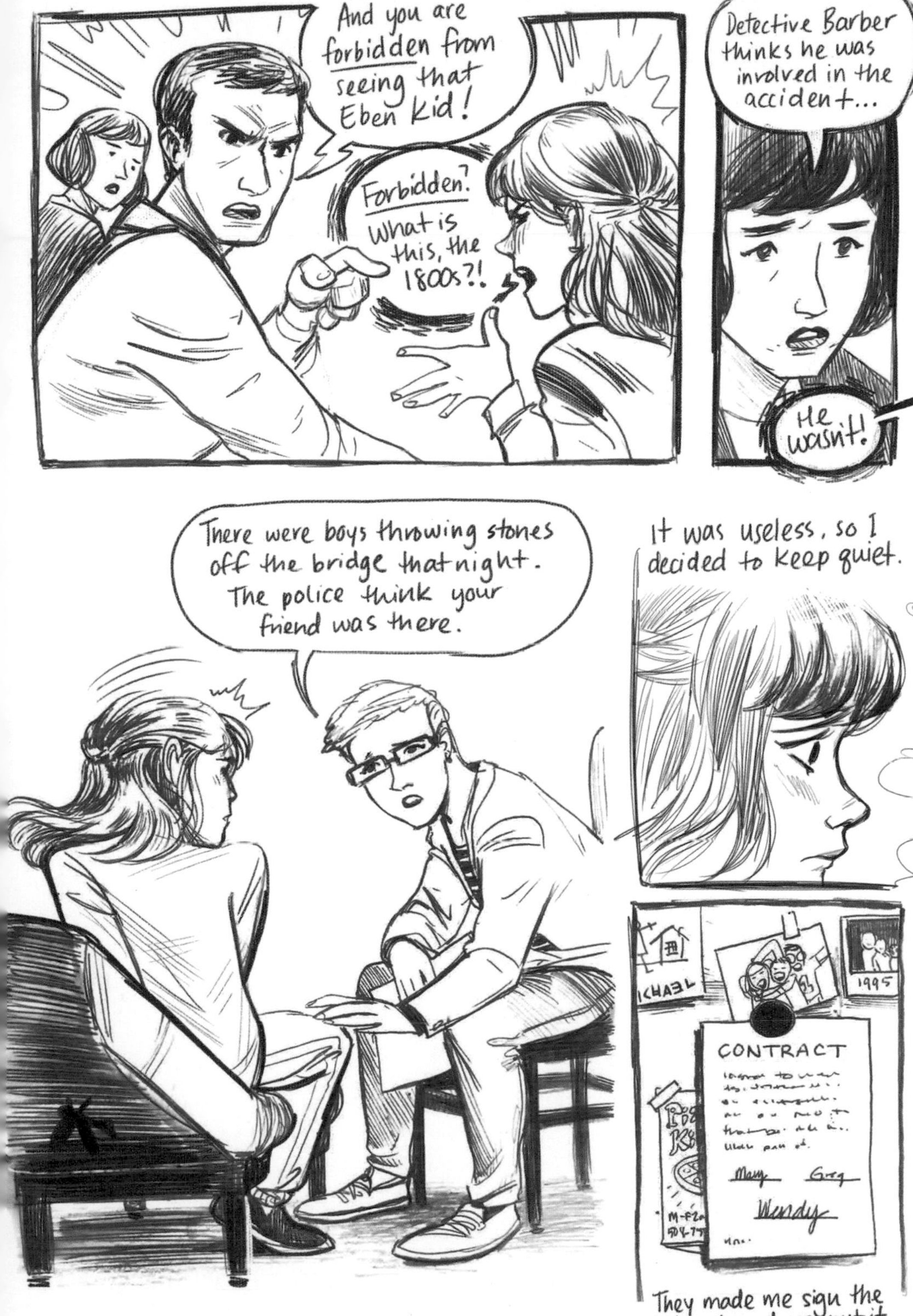
And you are forbidden from seeing that Eben kid!
Forbidden? What is this, the 1800s?!
Detective Barber thinks he was involved in the accident...
He wasn't!
There were boys throwing stones off the bridge that night. The police think your friend was there.
It was useless, so I decided to keep quiet.
ICHAEL
1995
CONTRACT
Mary
Greg
Wendy
They made me sign the contract and we put it on the fridge, like that makes things official.

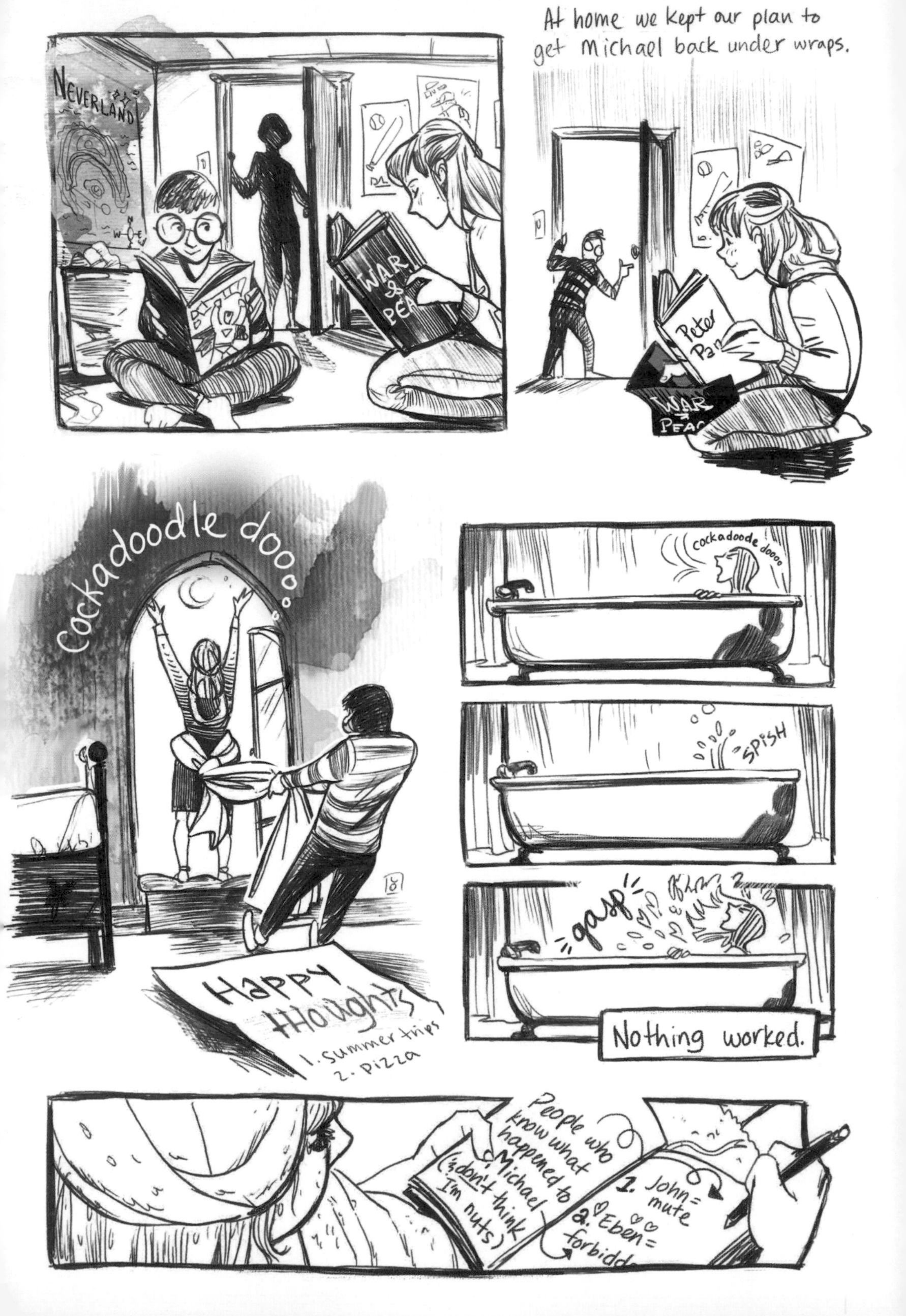
NEVERLAND
WAR & PEA
At home we kept our plan to get Michael back under wraps.
Peter Pan
WAR & PEAC
cockadoodle doooo
Happy Thoughts
1. summer trips
2. pizza
cockadoode doooo
SPISH
gasp
Nothing worked.
People who know what happened to Michael (& don't think I'm nuts)
1. John = mute
2. Eben = forbidd

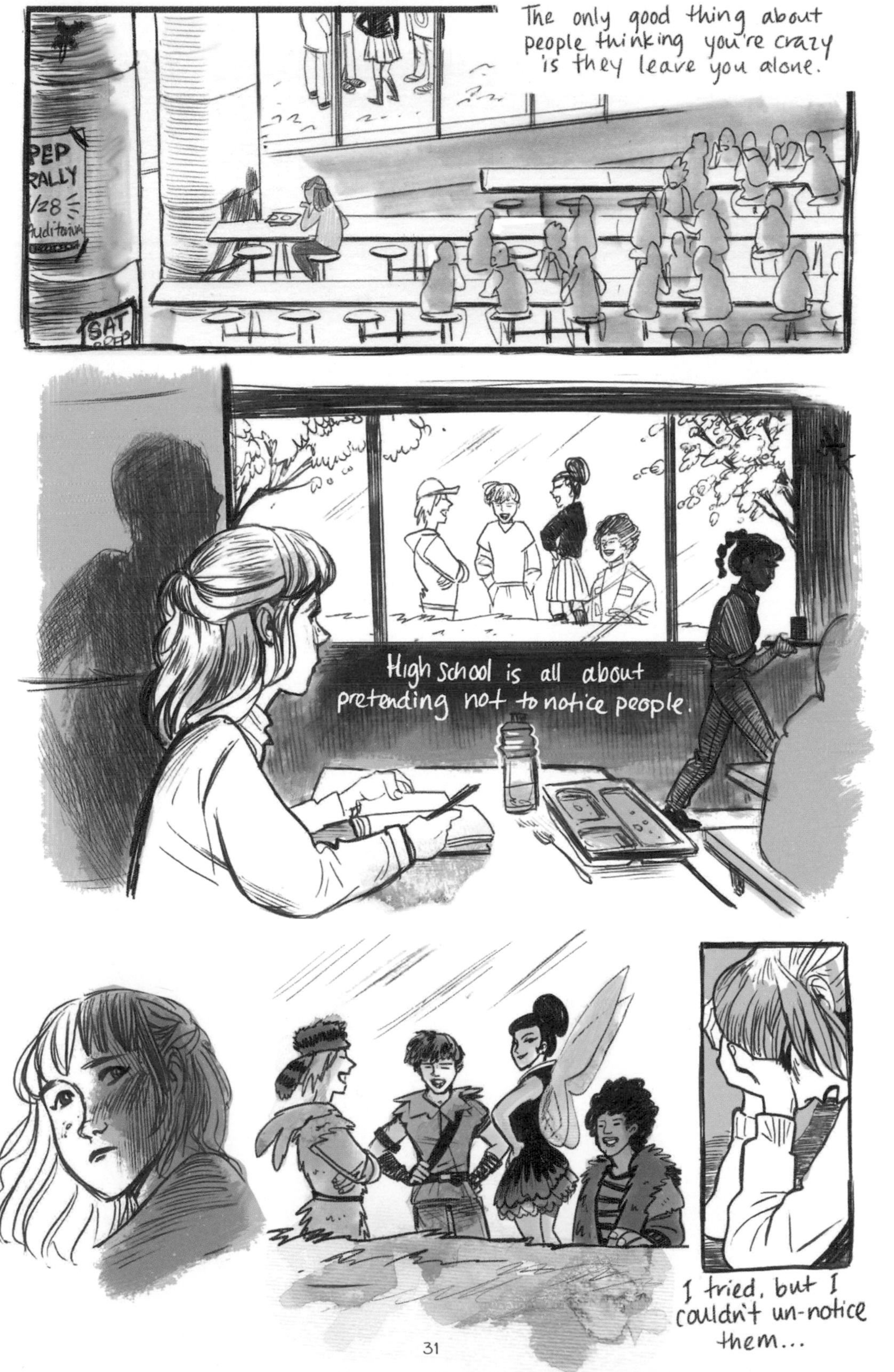
The only good thing about people thinking you're crazy is they leave you alone.
PEP RALLY 1/28 Auditorium
SAT PREP
High School is all about pretending not to notice people.
I tried, but I couldn't un-notice them...

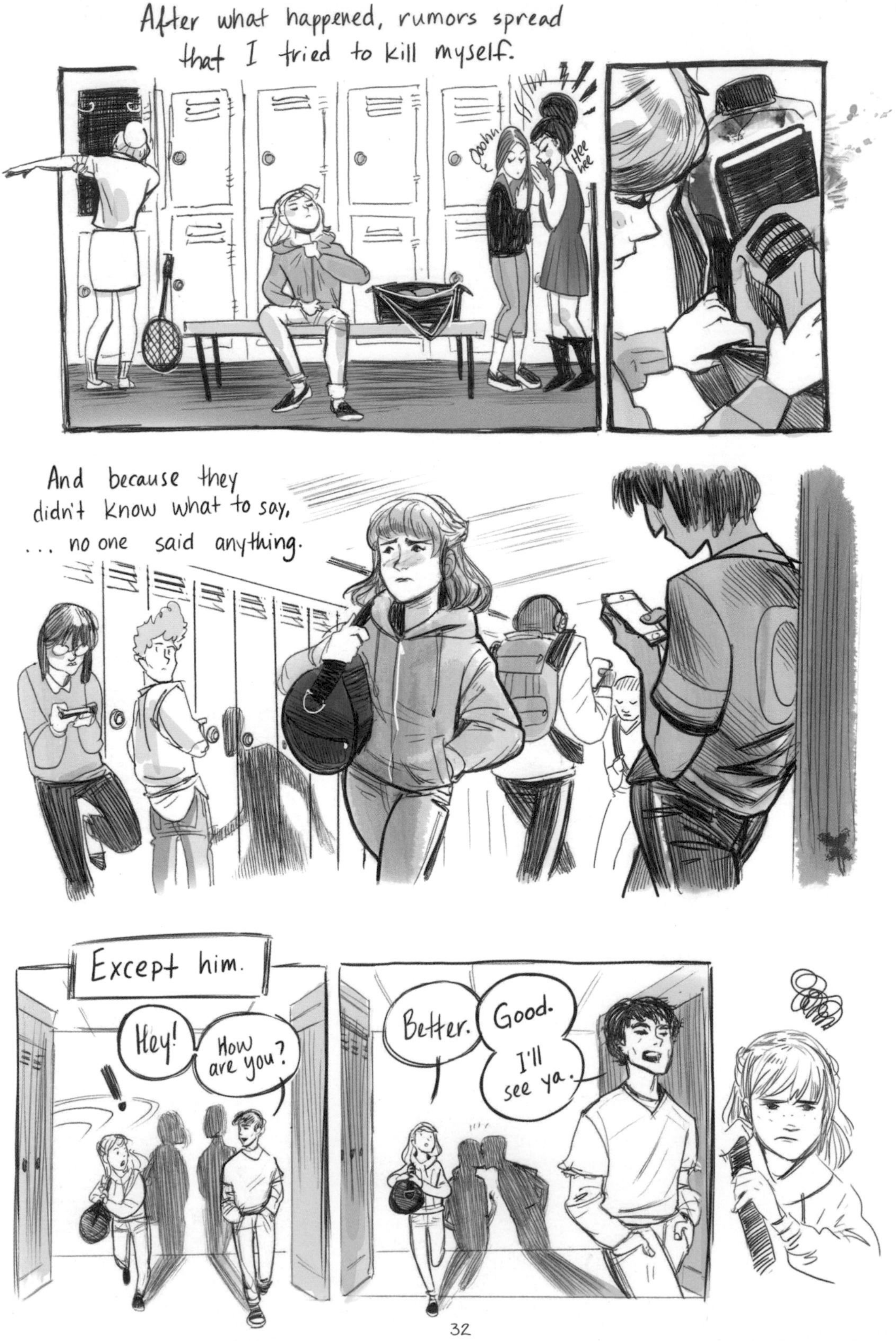
After what happened, rumors spread that I tried to kill myself.
Hee hee
And because they didn't know what to say, ... no one said anything.
Except him.
Hey!
How are you?
Better.
Good.
I'll see ya.

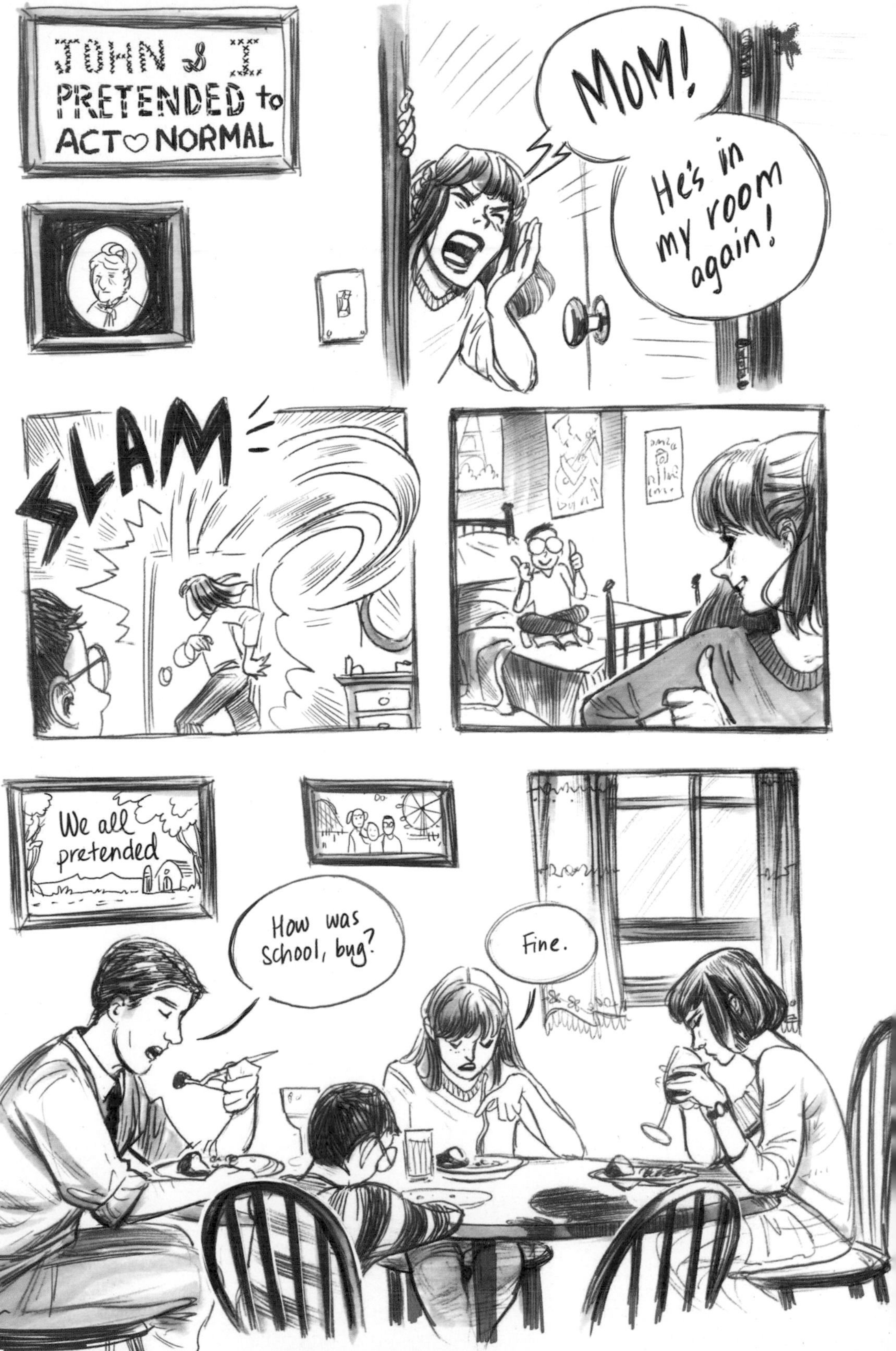

JOHN & I PRETENDED to ACT NORMAL
MOM!
He's in my room again!
SLAM
We all pretended
How was school, bug?
Fine.

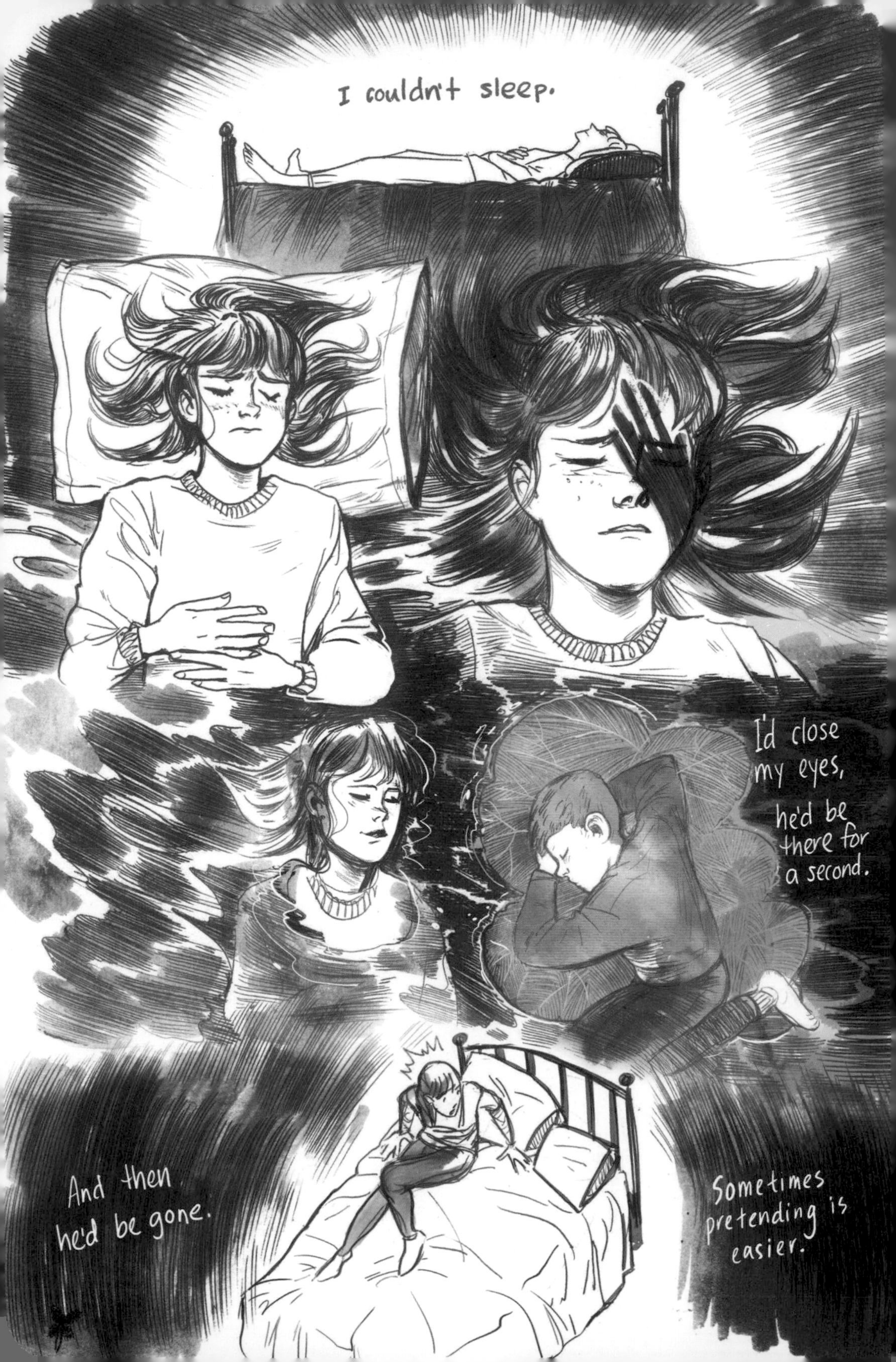
I couldn't sleep.
I'd close my eyes,
he'd be there for a second.
And then he'd be gone.
Sometimes pretending is easier.

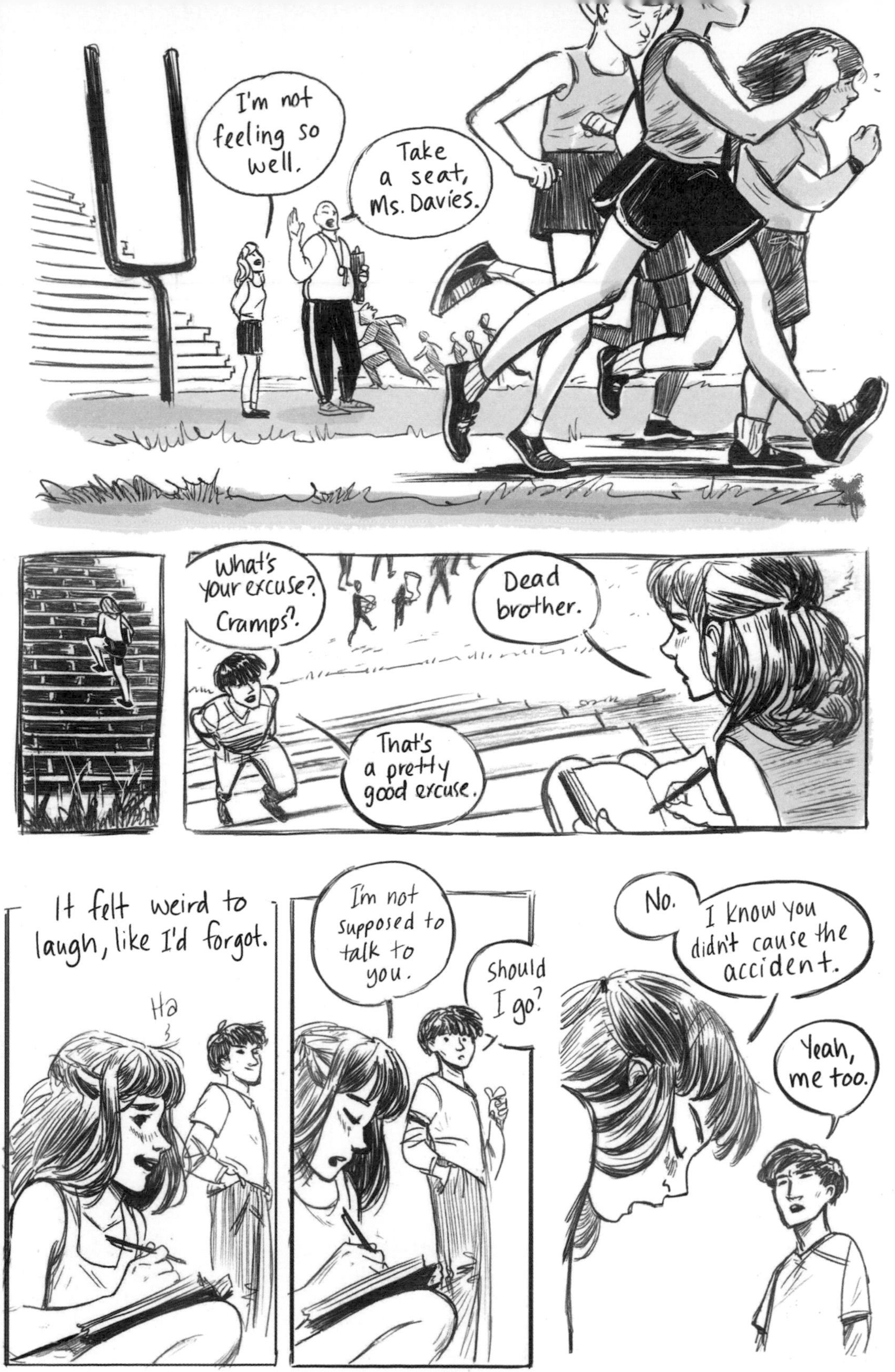
I'm not feeling so well.
Take a seat, Ms. Davies.
What's your excuse? Cramps?
Dead brother.
That's a pretty good excuse.
It felt weird to laugh, like I'd forgot.
Ha
I'm not supposed to talk to you.
Should I go?
No.
I know you didn't cause the accident.
Yeah, me too.

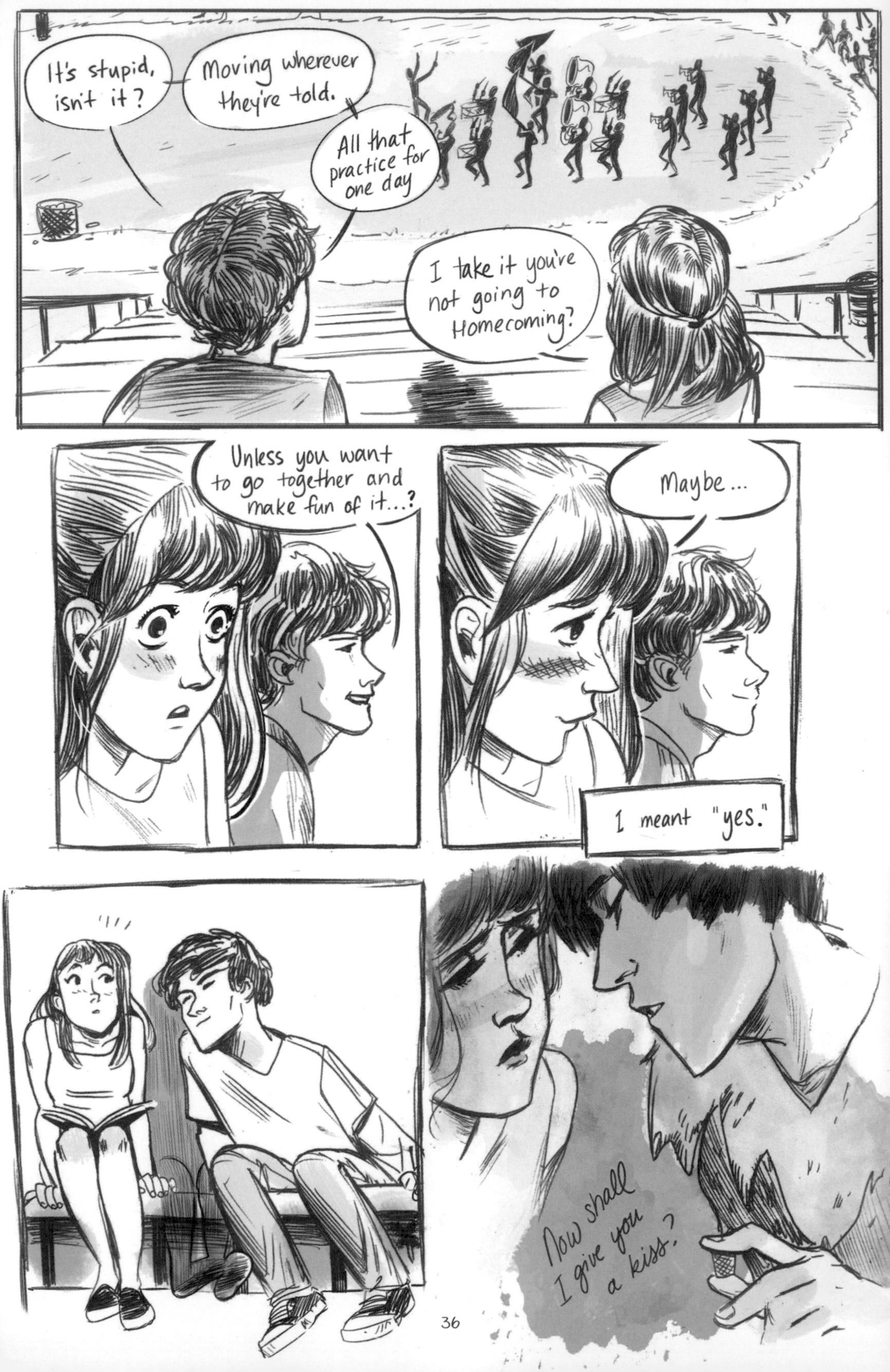
It's stupid, isn't it?
Moving wherever they're told.
All that practice for one day
I take it you're not going to Homecoming?
Unless you want to go together and make fun of it...?
Maybe...
I meant "yes."
Now shall I give you a kiss?

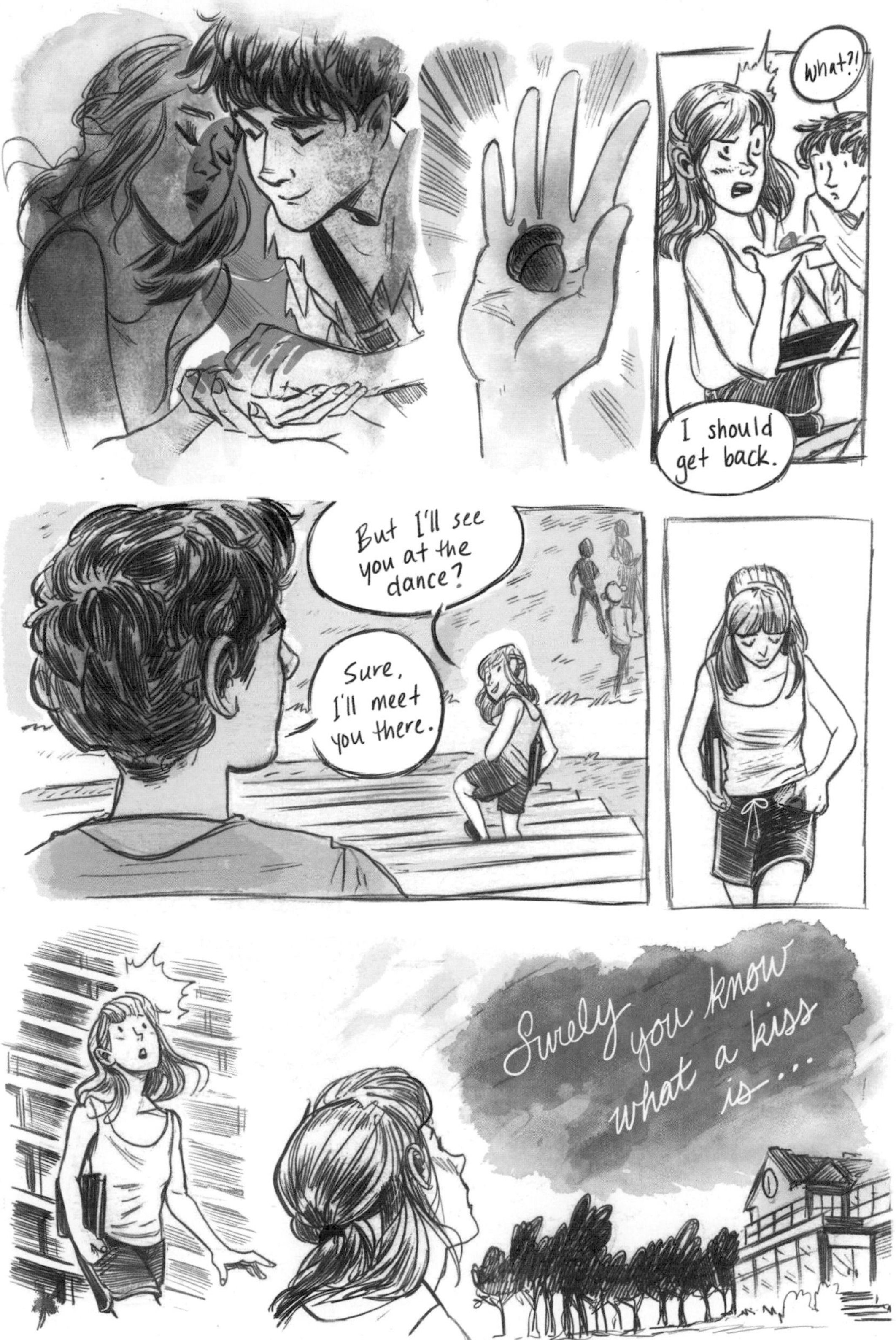
what?!
I should get back.
But I'll see you at the dance?
Sure, I'll meet you there.
Surely you know what a kiss is...

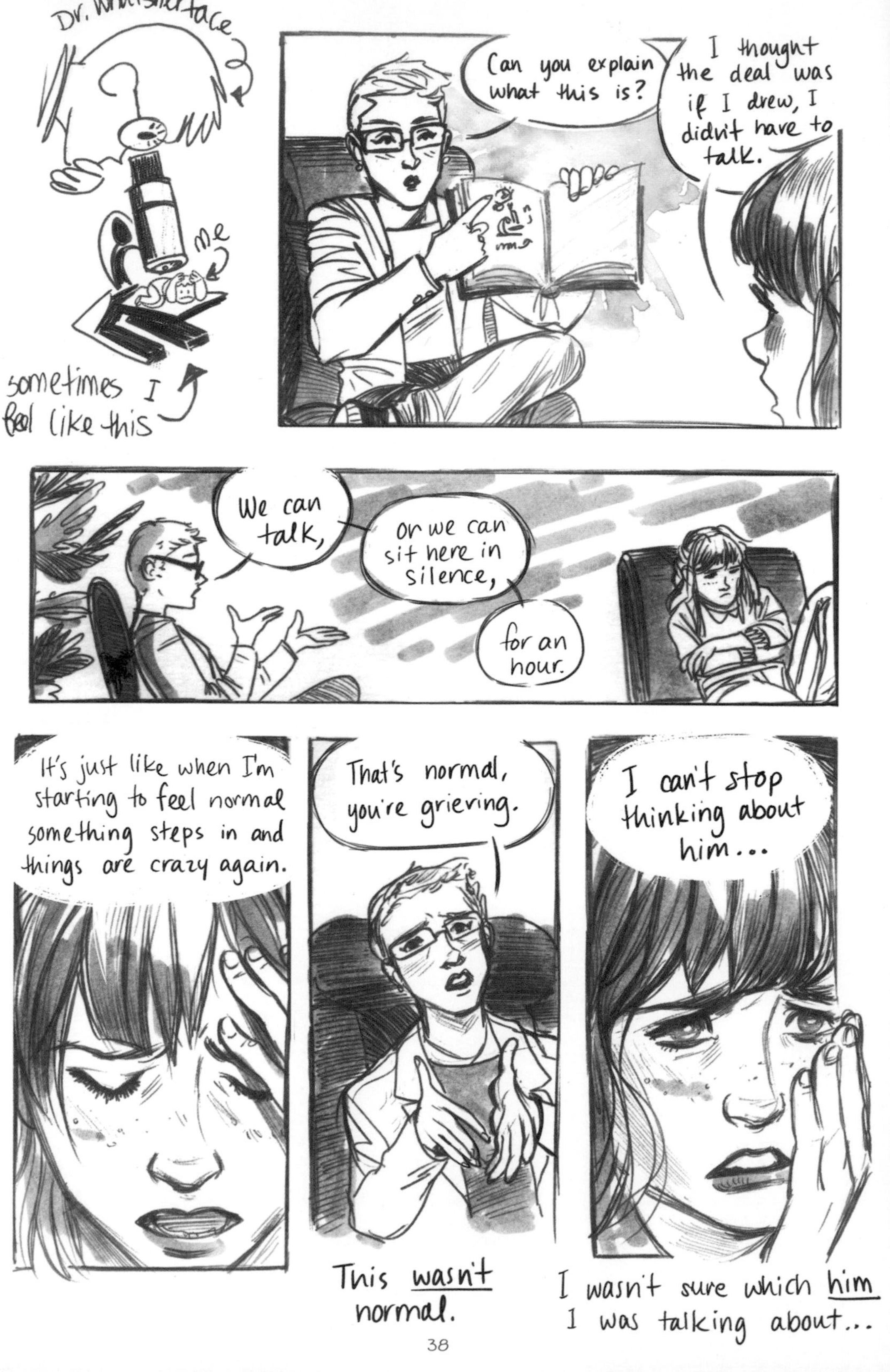
Dr. Whatsherface
me
sometimes I feel like this
Can you explain what this is?
I thought the deal was if I drew, I didn't have to talk.
We can talk,
or we can sit here in silence,
for an hour.
It's just like when I'm starting to feel normal something steps in and things are crazy again.
That's normal, you're grieving.
This wasn't normal.
I can't stop thinking about him...
I wasn't sure which him I was talking about...

They packed up all his things like he didn't exist.

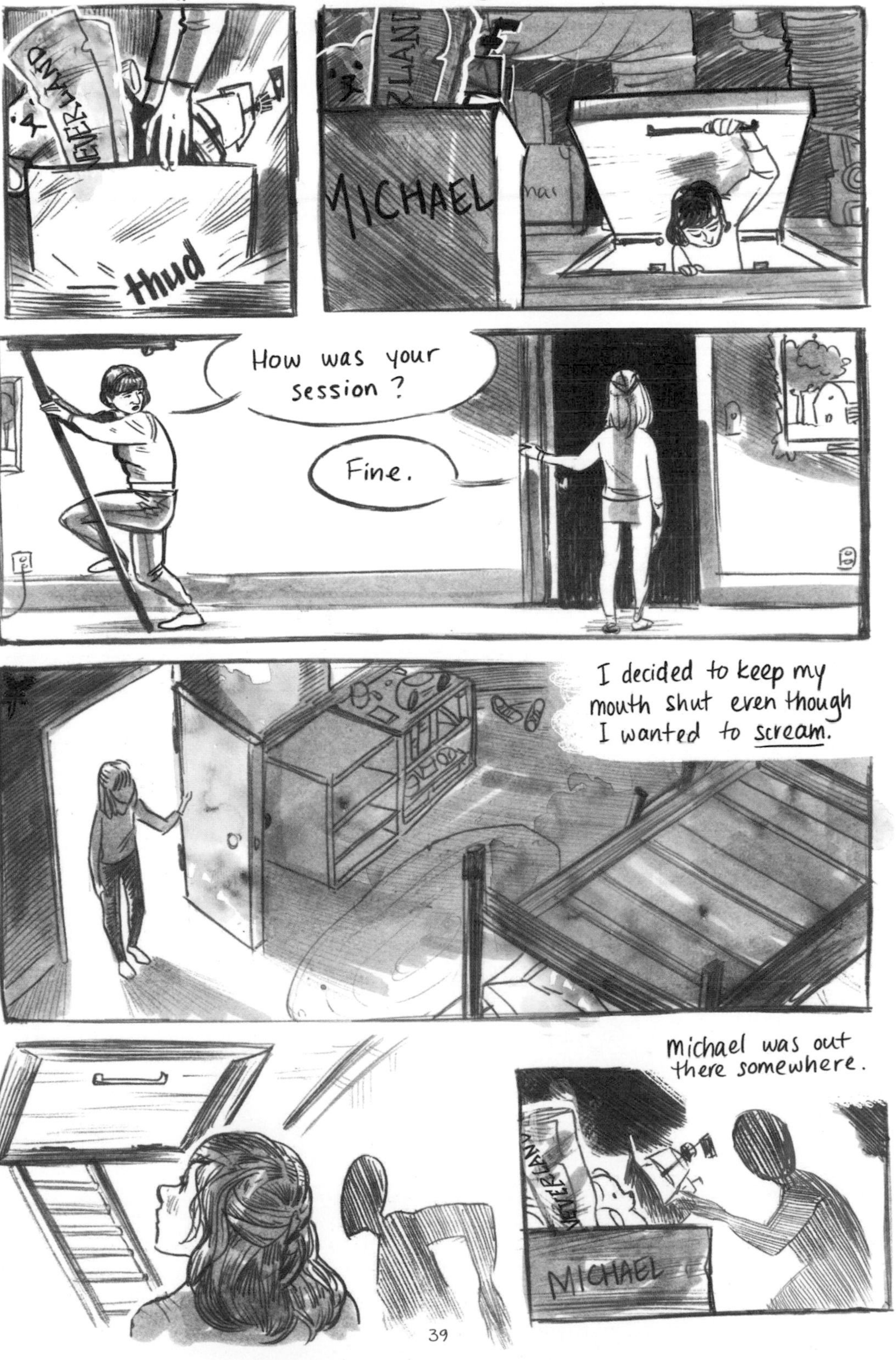
NEVERLAND
thud
MICHAEL
How was your session?
Fine.
I decided to keep my mouth shut even though I wanted to scream.
Michael was out there somewhere.
NEVERLAND
MICHAEL

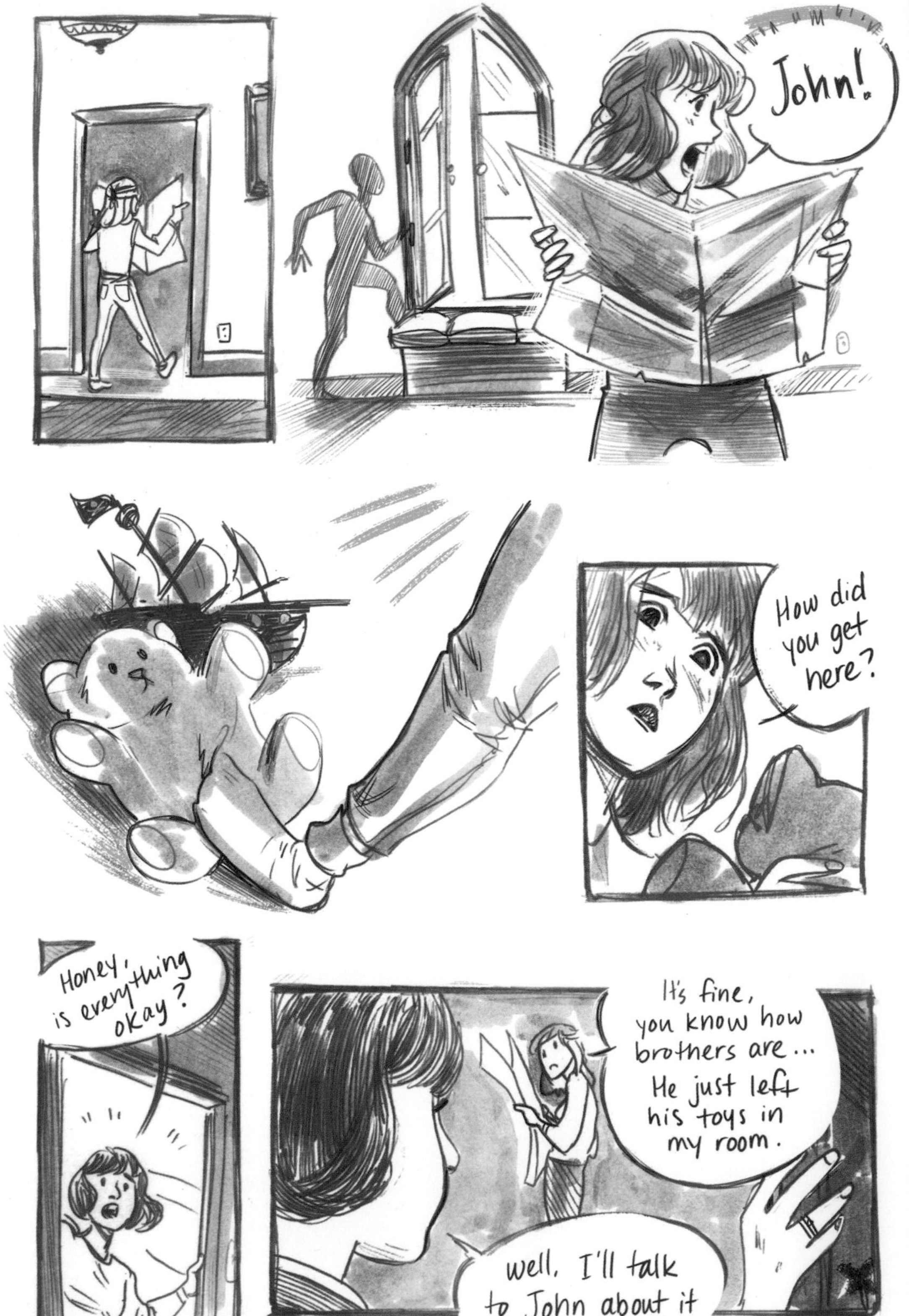
John!
How did you get here?
Honey, is everything okay?
It's fine, you know how brothers are... He just left his toys in my room.
well. I'll talk to John about it

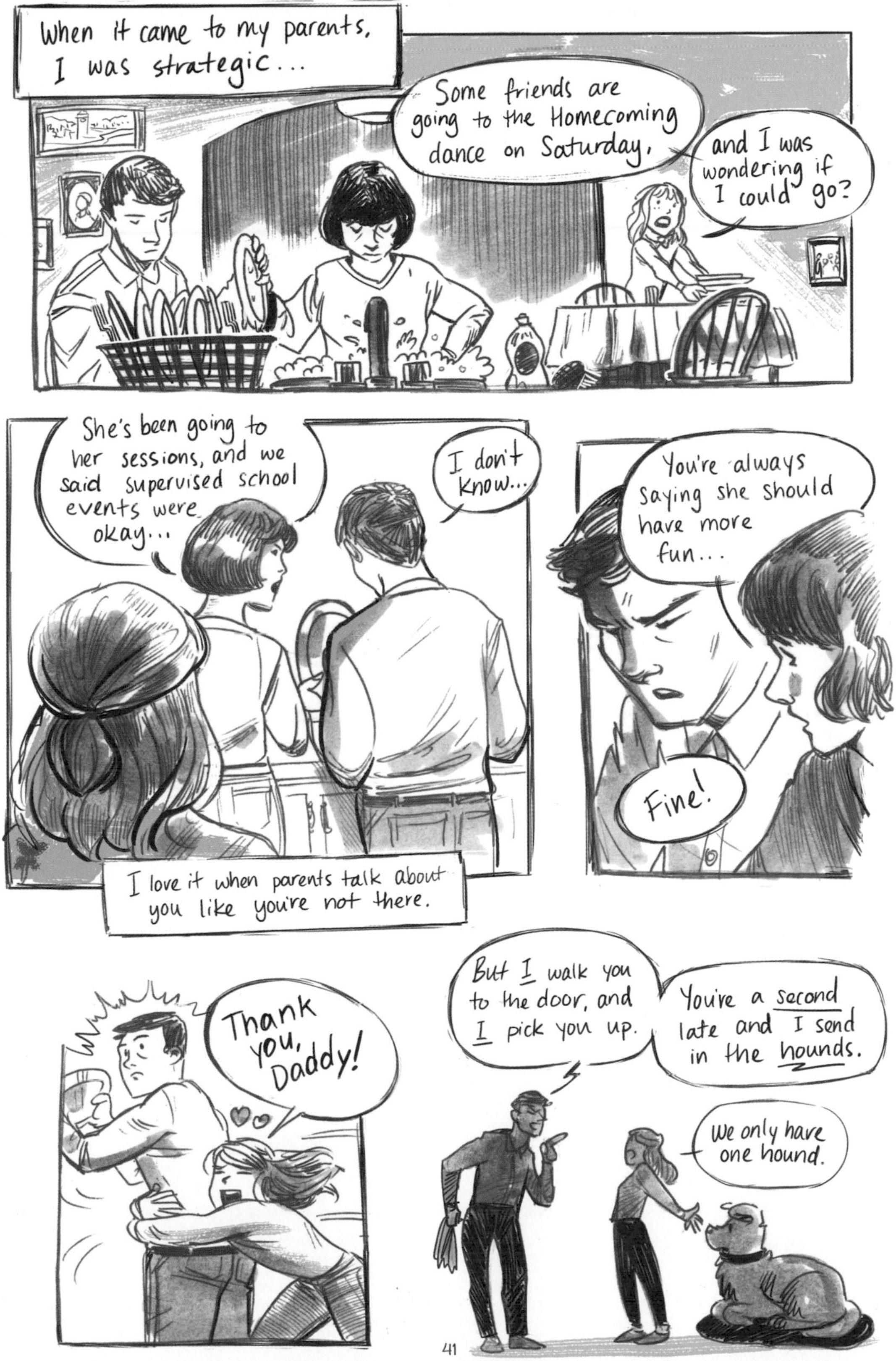
When it came to my parents, I was strategic...
Some friends are going to the Homecoming dance on Saturday,
and I was wondering if I could go?
She's been going to her sessions, and we said supervised school events were okay...
I don't know...
You're always saying she should have more fun...
Fine!
I love it when parents talk about you like you're not there.
Thank you, Daddy!
But I walk you to the door, and I pick you up.
You're a second late and I send in the hounds.
We only have one hound.

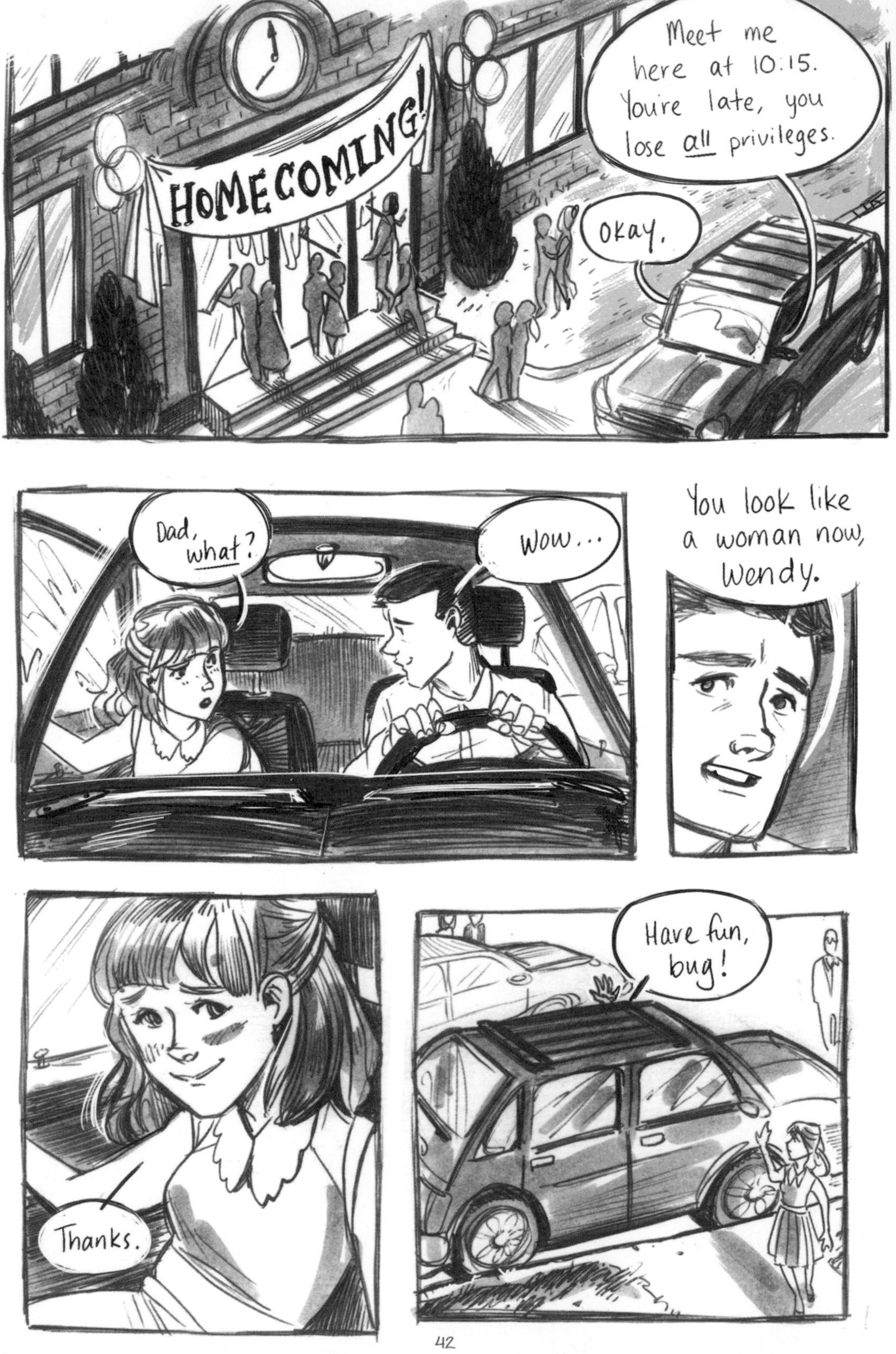
HOMECOMING!
Meet me here at 10:15. You're late, you lose all privileges.
Okay.
Dad, what?
Wow...
You look like a woman now, Wendy.
Thanks.
Have fun, bug!

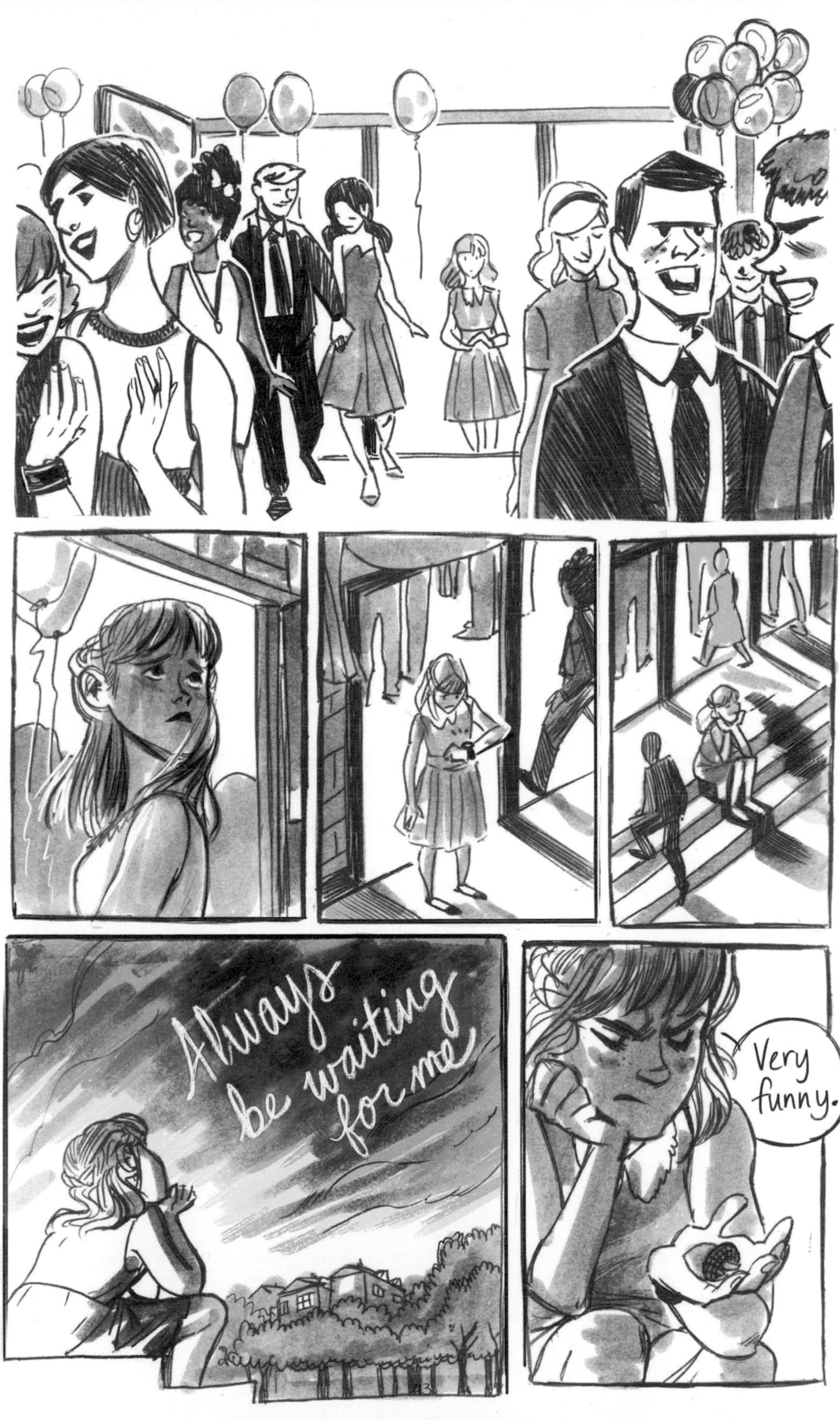
Always be waiting for me
Very funny.

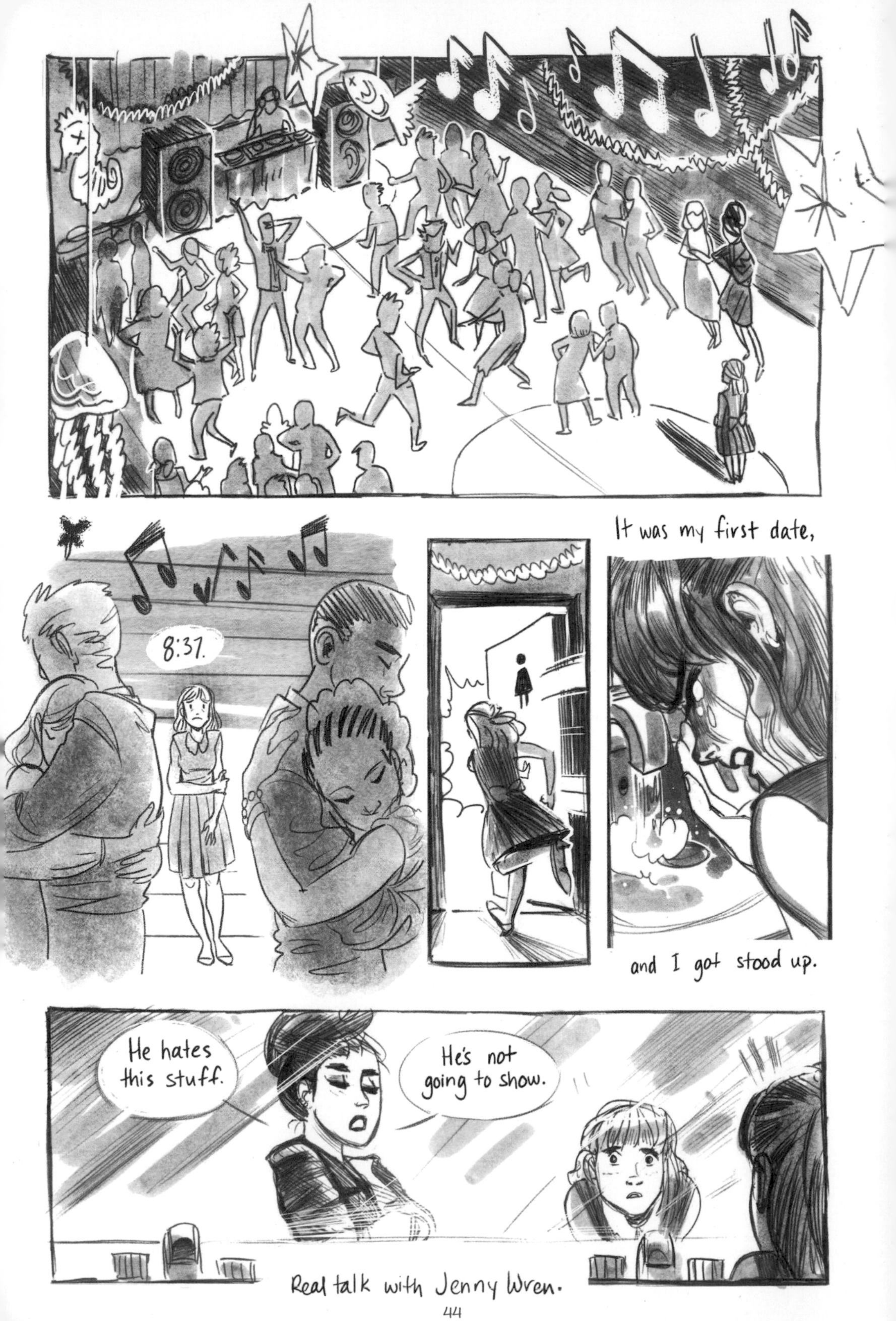
8:31.
It was my first date,
and I got stood up.
He hates this stuff.
He's not going to show.
Real talk with Jenny Wren.

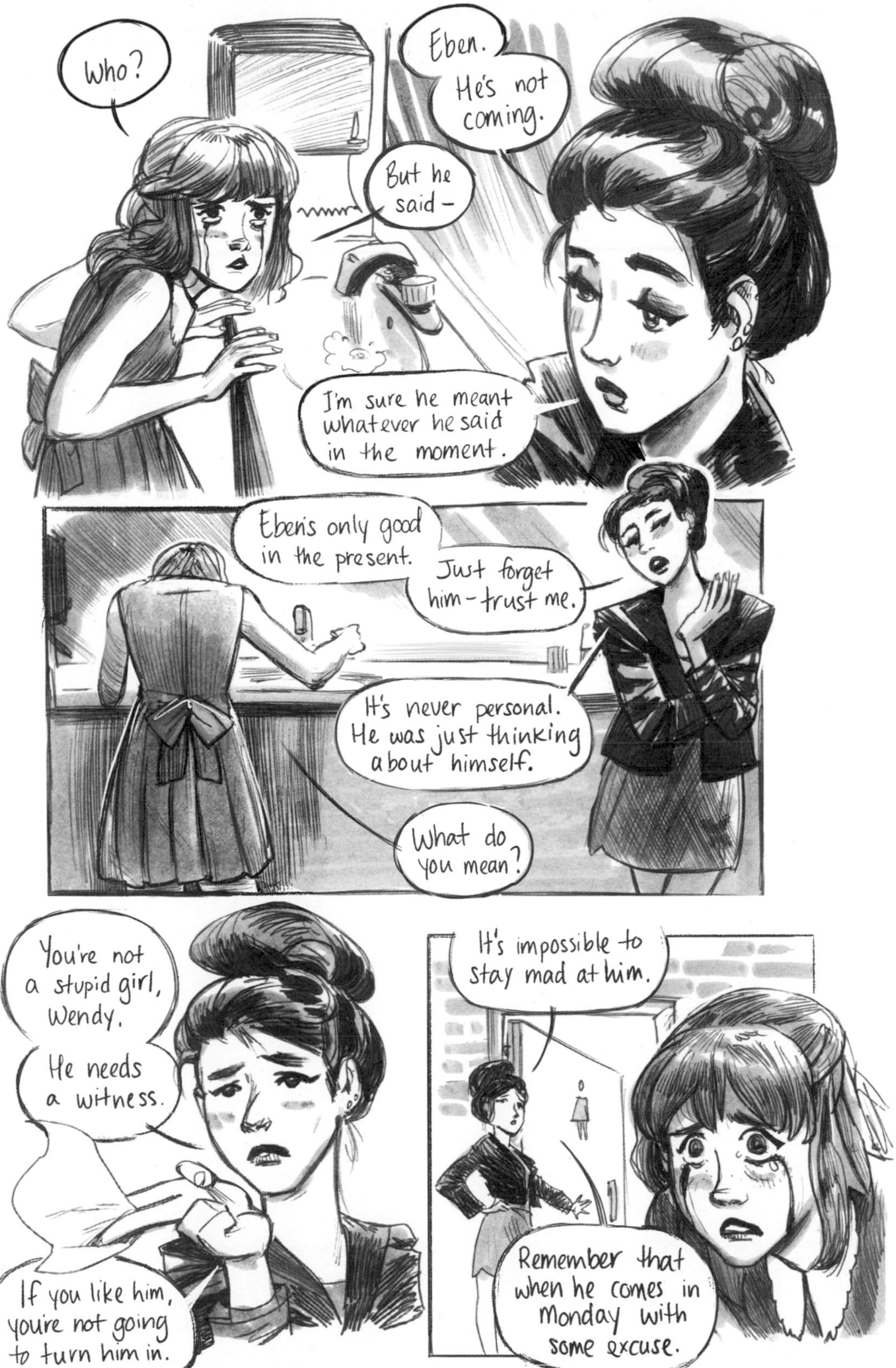
Who?
Eben.
He's not coming.
But he said -
I'm sure he meant whatever he said in the moment.
Eben's only good in the present.
Just forget him - trust me.
It's never personal. He was just thinking about himself.
What do you mean?
You're not a stupid girl, Wendy.
He needs a witness.
If you like him, you're not going to turn him in.
It's impossible to stay mad at him.
Remember that when he comes in Monday with some excuse.

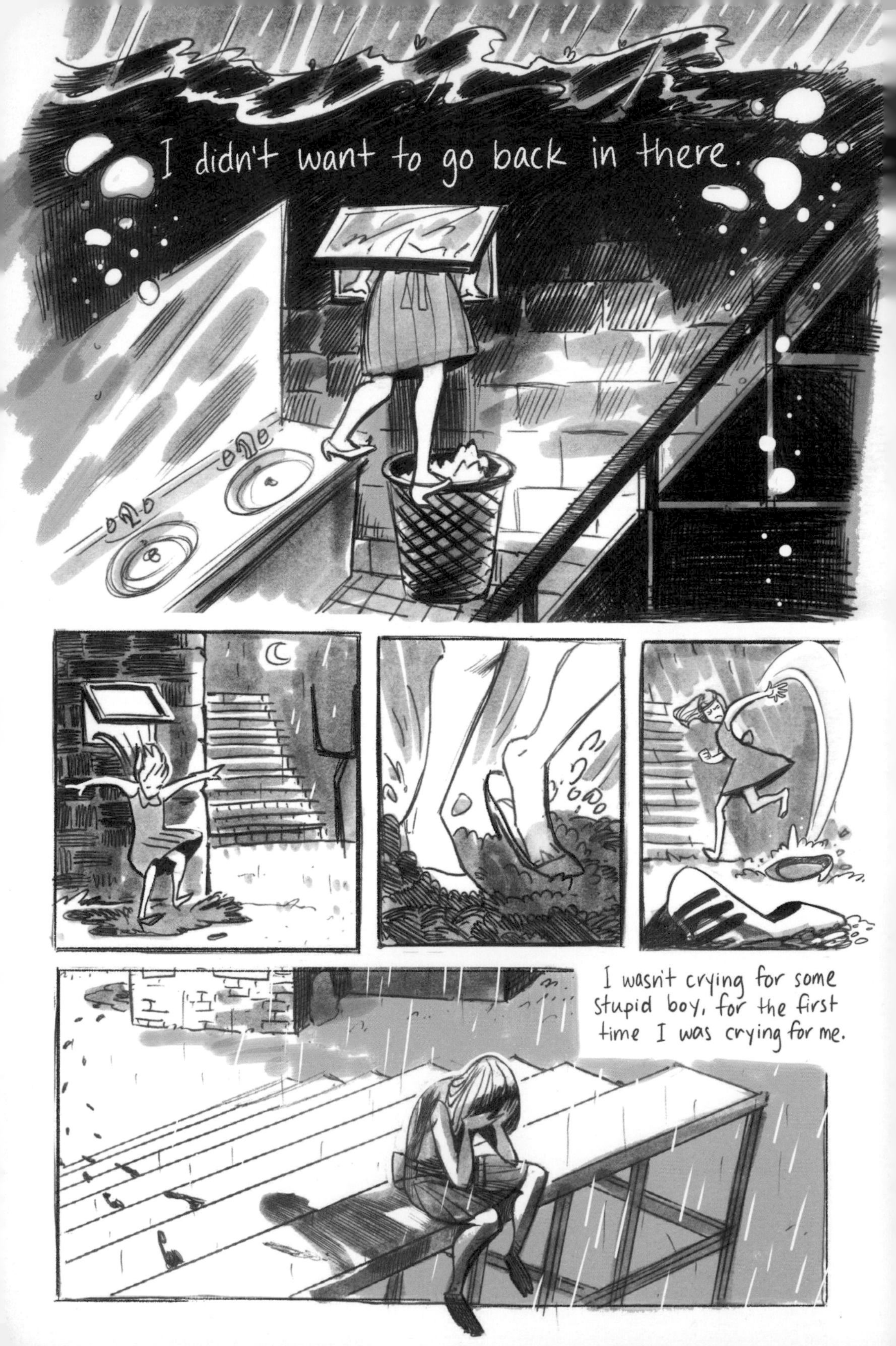
I didn't want to go back in there.
I wasn't crying for some stupid boy, for the first time I was crying for me.

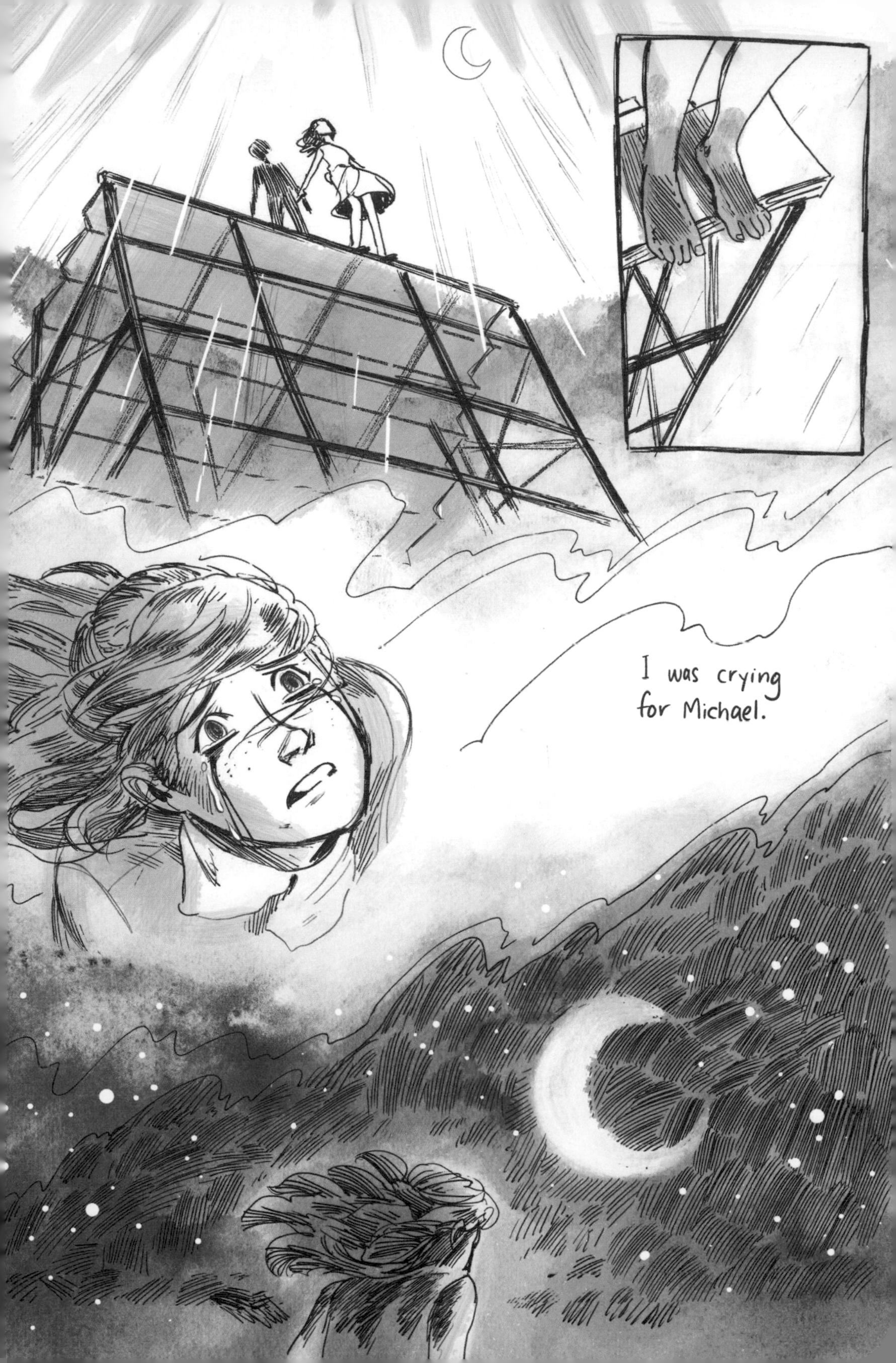
I was crying for Michael.

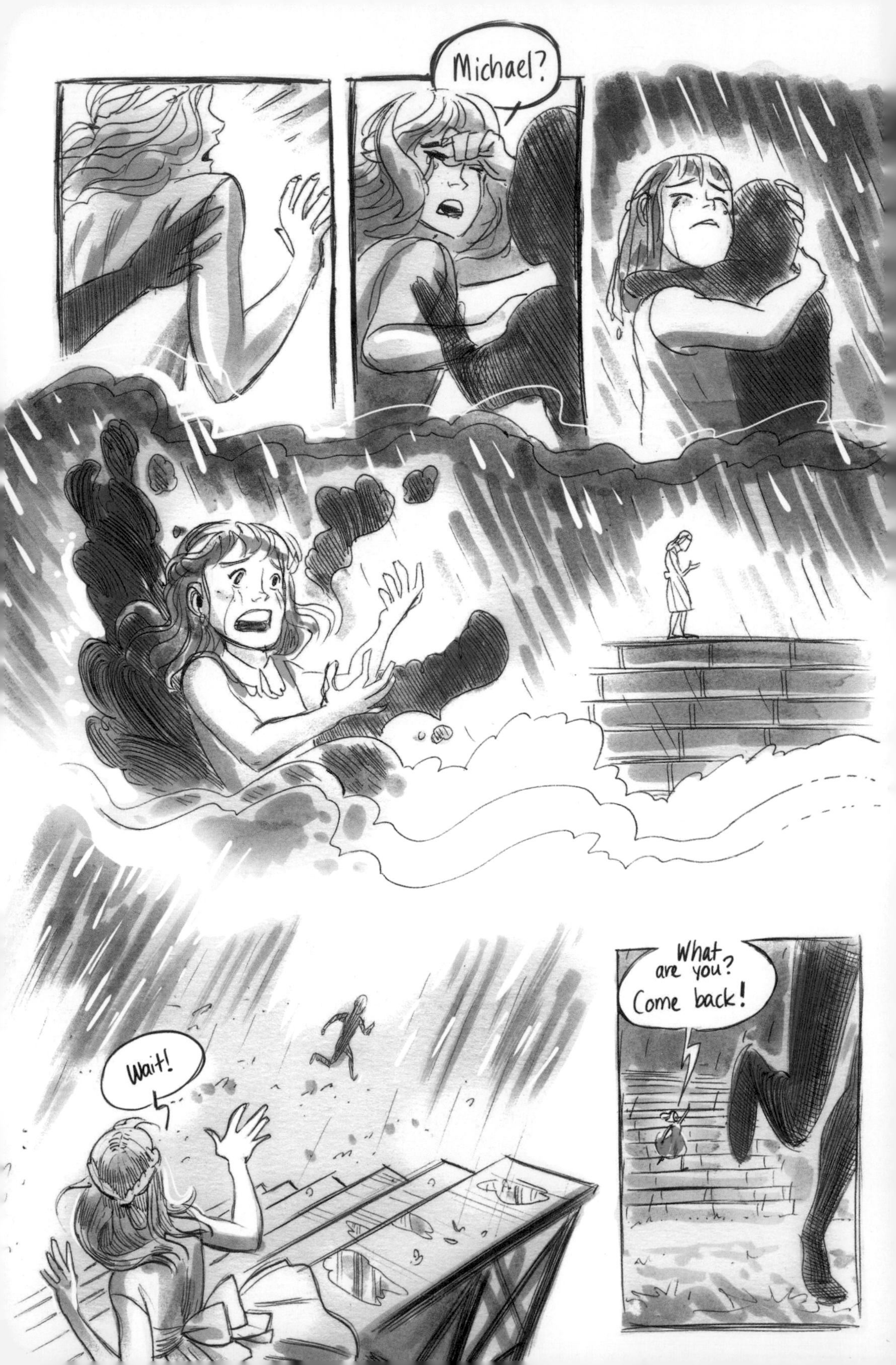
Michael?
Wait!
What are you? Come back!

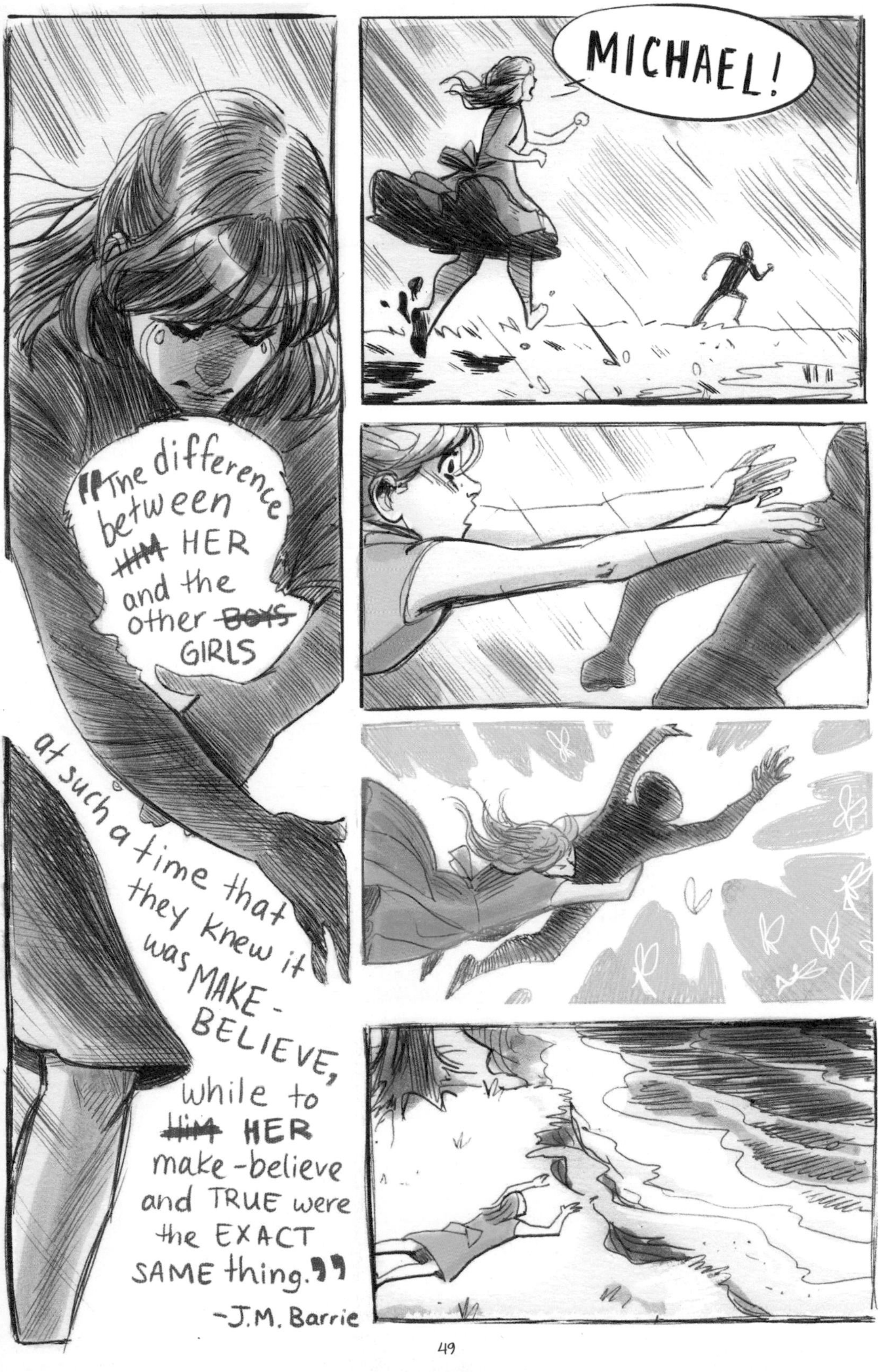
"The difference between ~~HIM~~ HER and the other ~~BOYS~~ GIRLS
at such a time that they knew it was MAKE-BELIEVE, while to ~~HIM~~ HER make-believe and TRUE were the EXACT SAME thing."
-J.M. Barrie
MICHAEL!

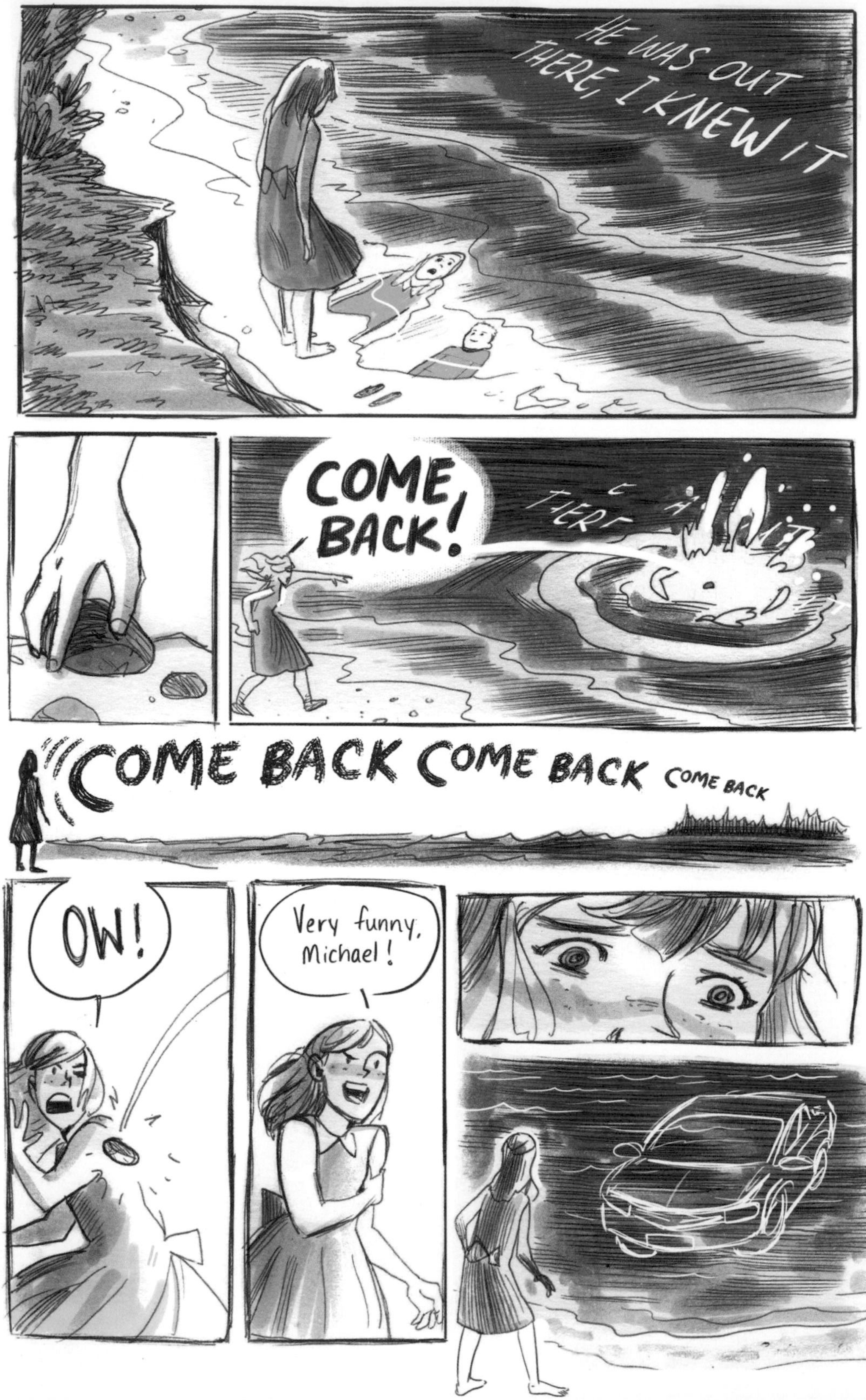

HE WAS OUT THERE, I KNEW IT
COME BACK!
COME BACK COME BACK COME BACK
OW!
Very funny, Michael!

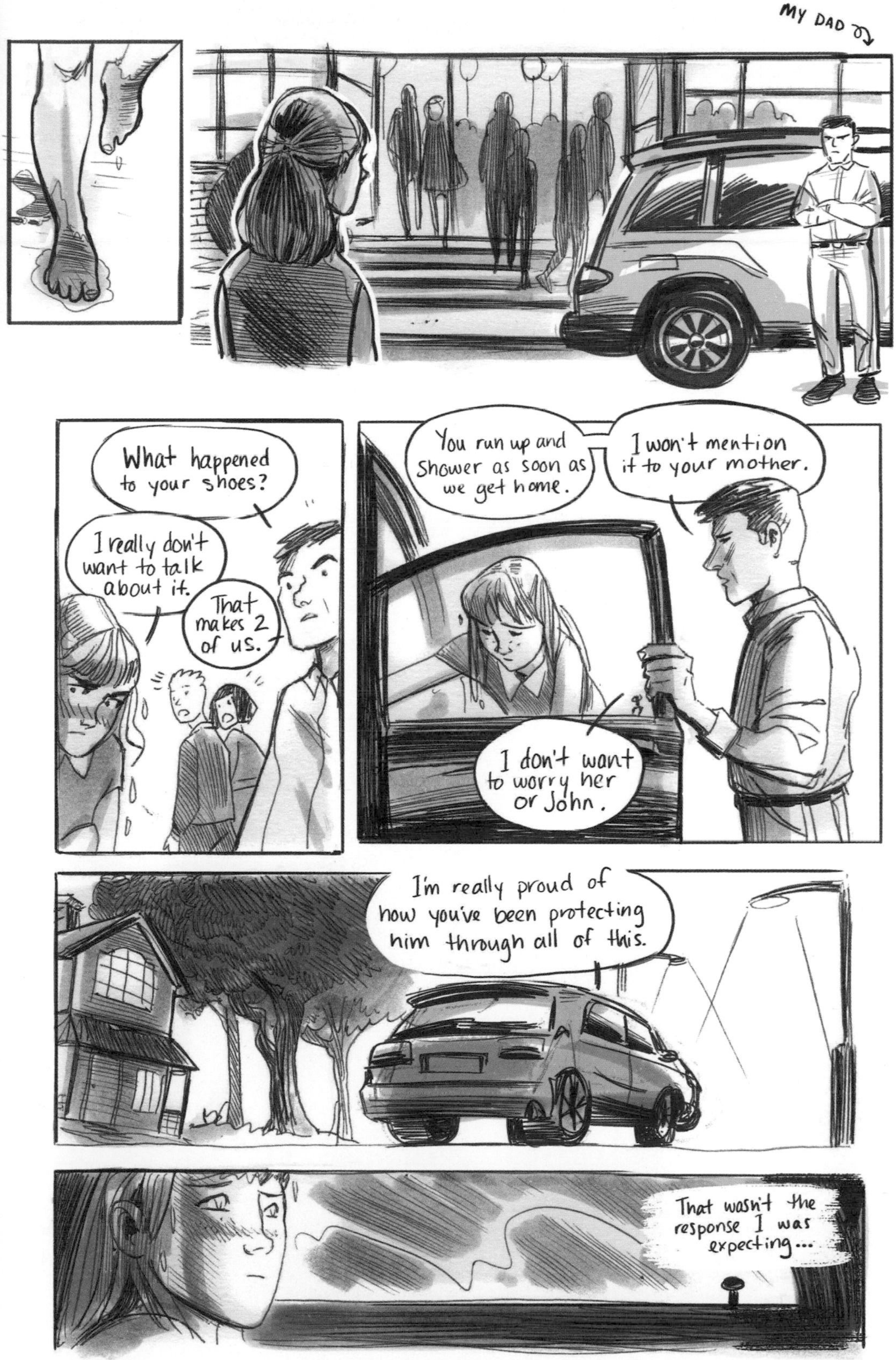
MY DAD
What happened to your shoes?
I really don't want to talk about it.
That makes 2 of us.
You run up and shower as soon as we get home.
I won't mention it to your mother.
I don't want to worry her or John.
I'm really proud of how you've been protecting him through all of this.
That wasn't the response I was expecting...

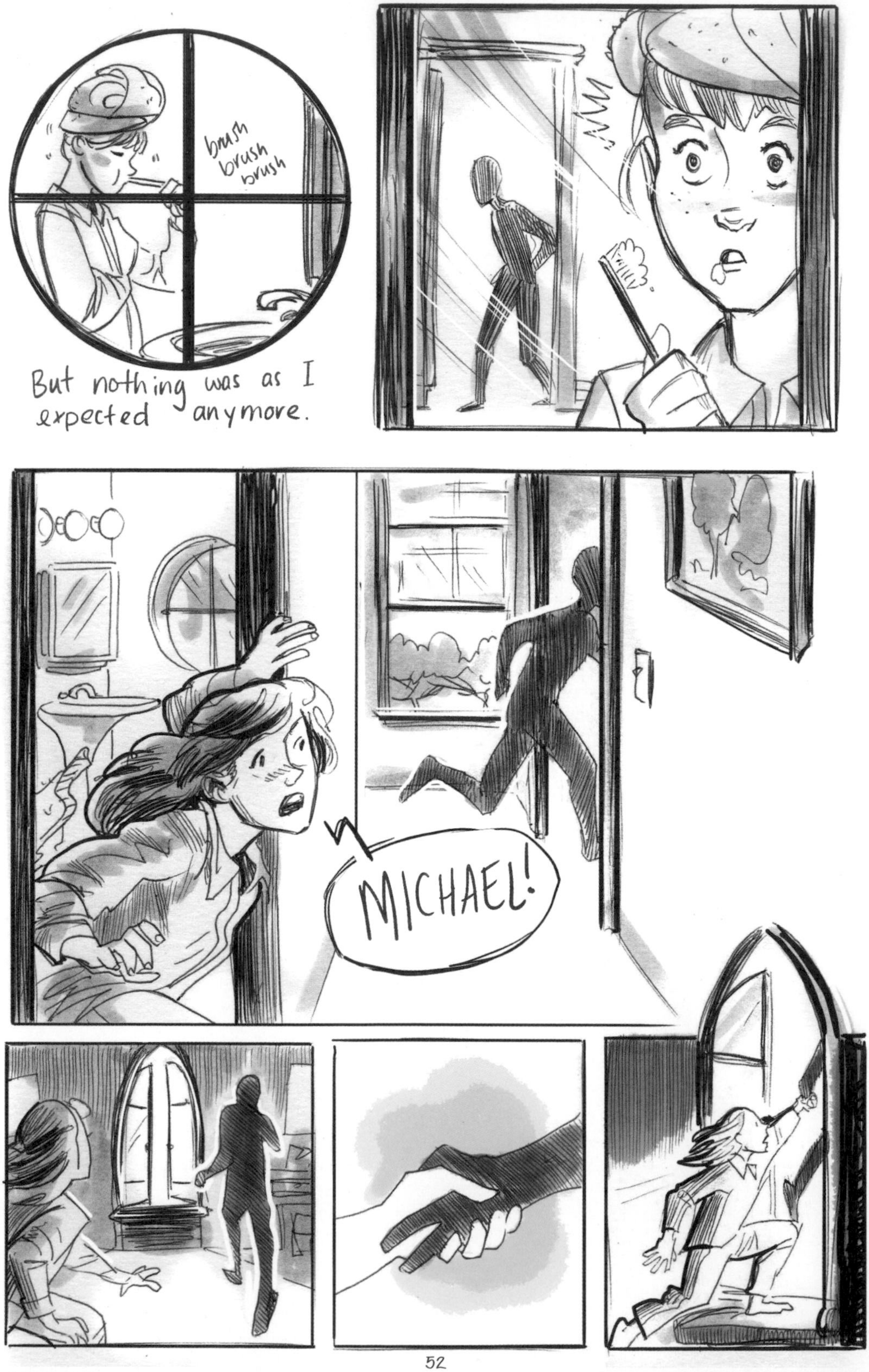
brush
brush
brush
But nothing was as I expected anymore.
MICHAEL!

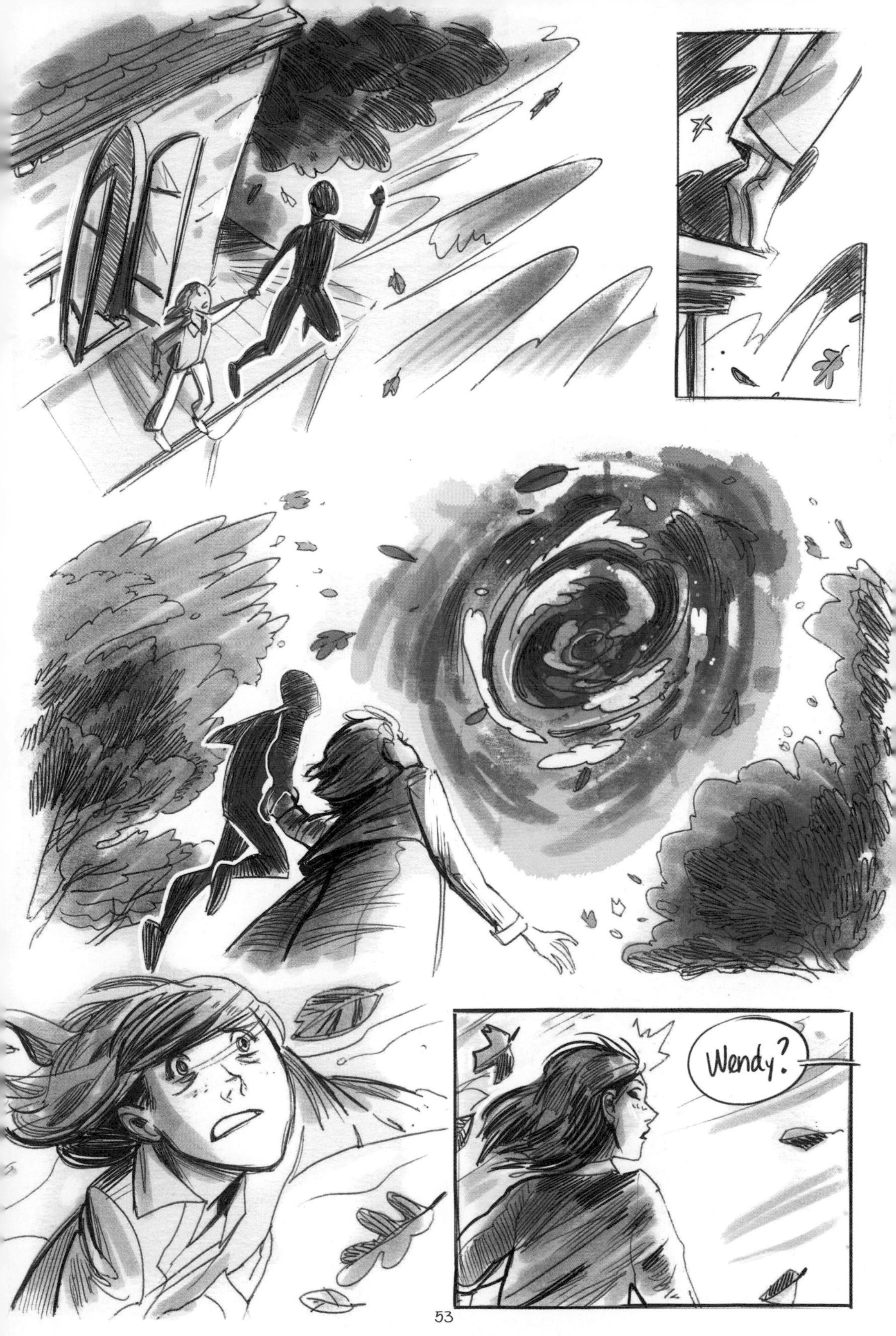
Wendy?

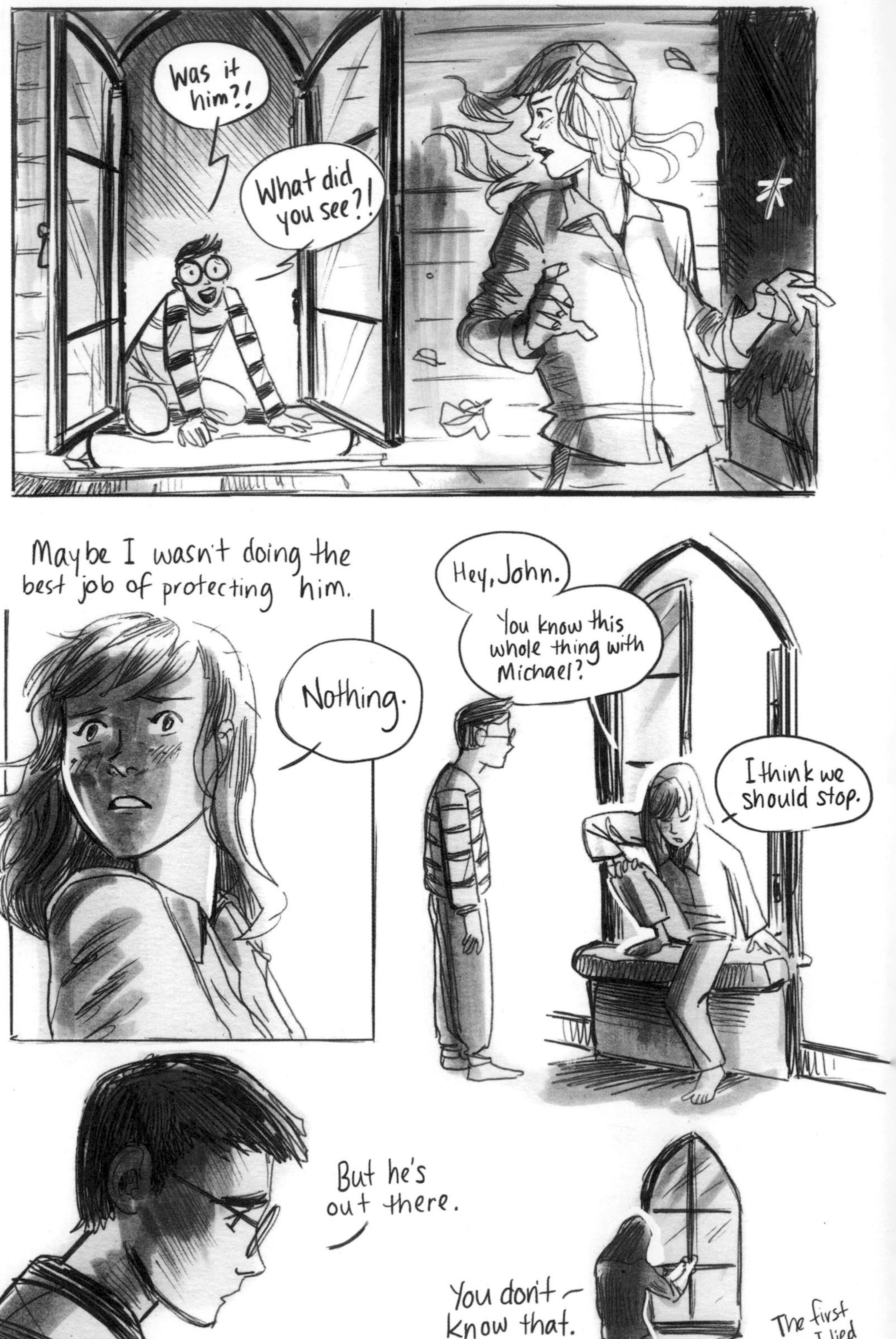
Was it him?!
What did you see?!
Maybe I wasn't doing the best job of protecting him.
Nothing.
Hey, John.
You know this whole thing with Michael?
I think we should stop.
But he's out there.
You don't—know that.
The first time I lied to my brother.

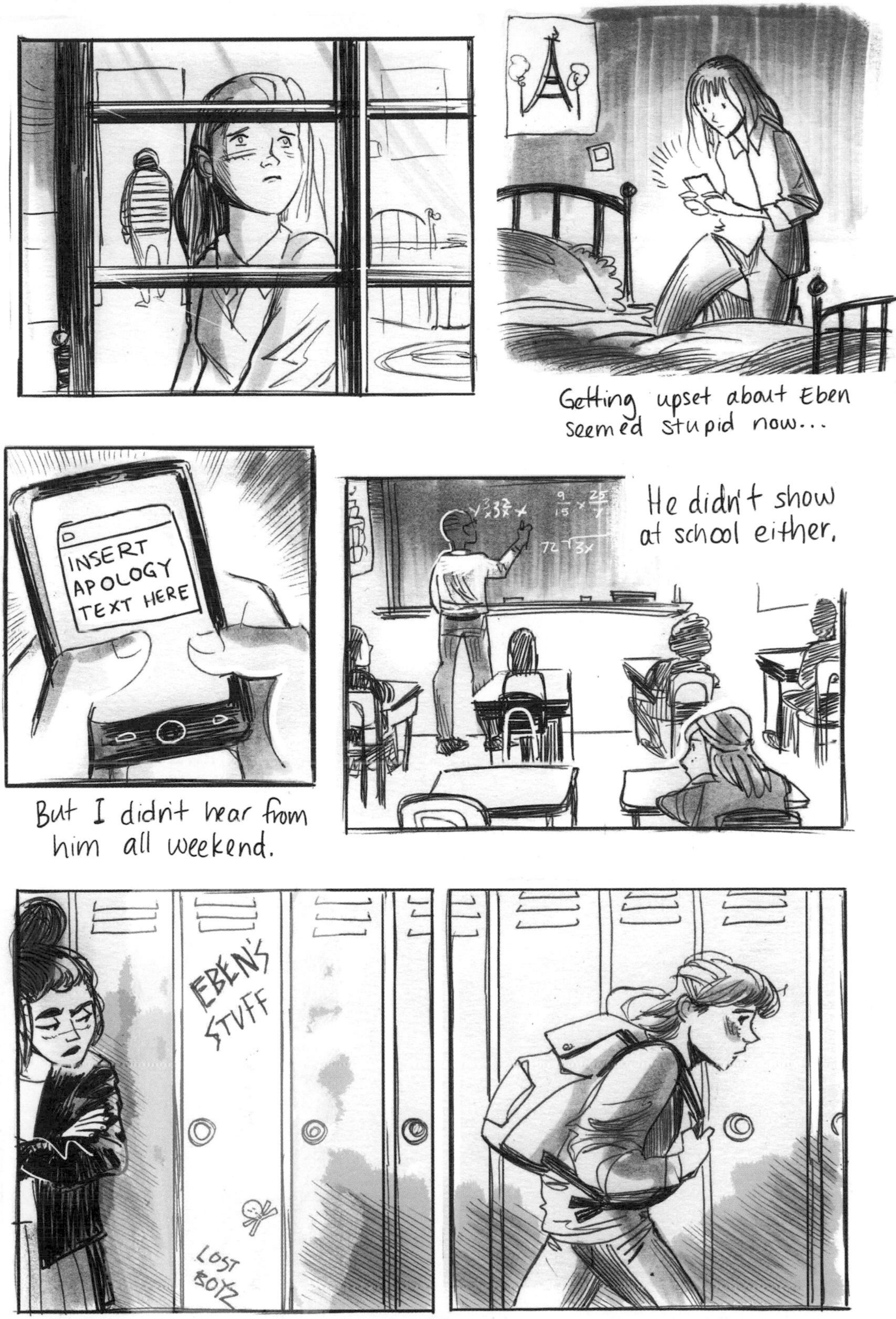
Getting upset about Eben seemed stupid now...
INSERT APOLOGY TEXT HERE
But I didn't hear from him all weekend.
He didn't show at school either.
EBEN'S STUFF
LOST BOYZ

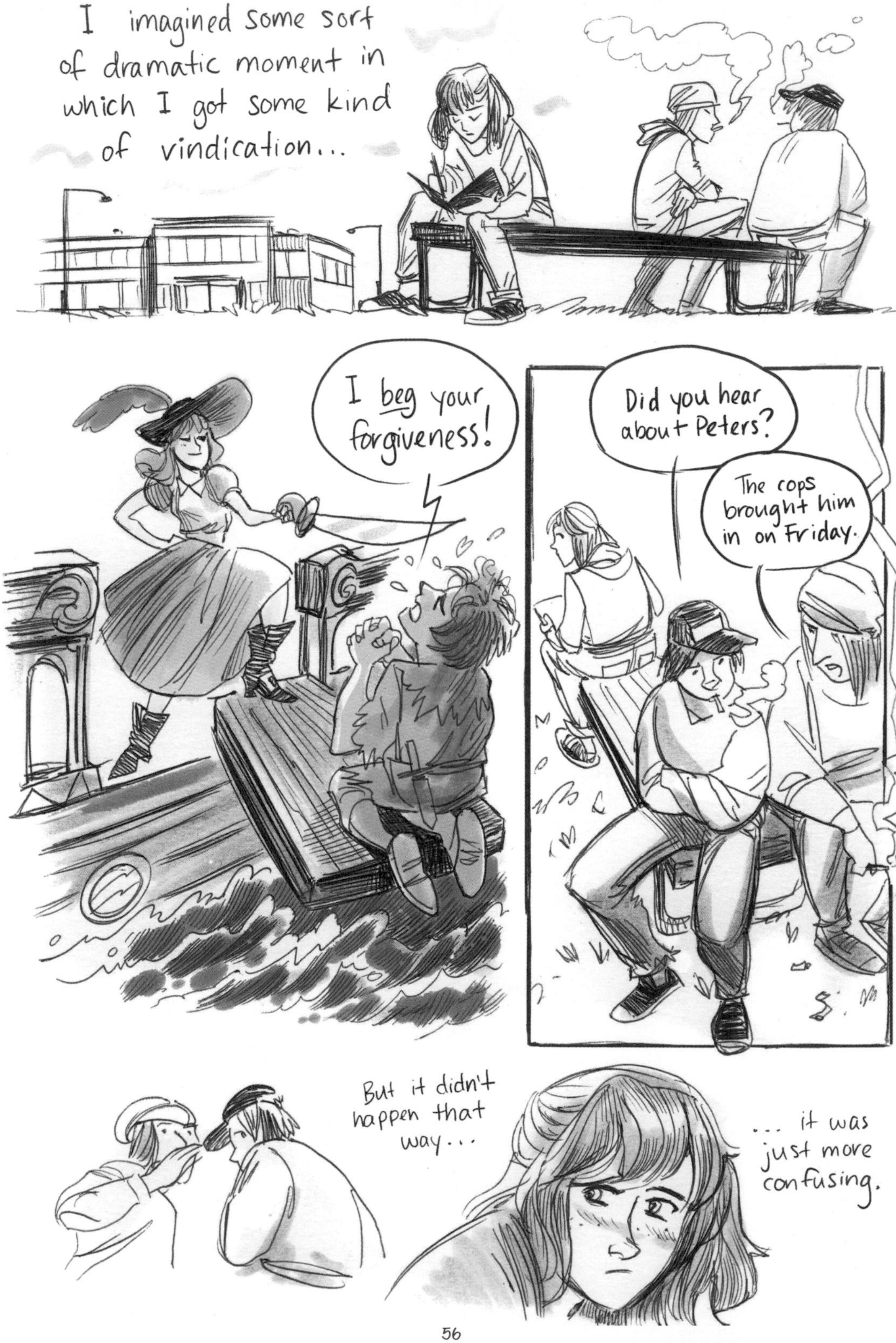
I imagined some sort of dramatic moment in which I got some kind of vindication...
I beg your forgiveness!
Did you hear about Peters?
The cops brought him in on Friday.
But it didn't happen that way...
... it was just more confusing.

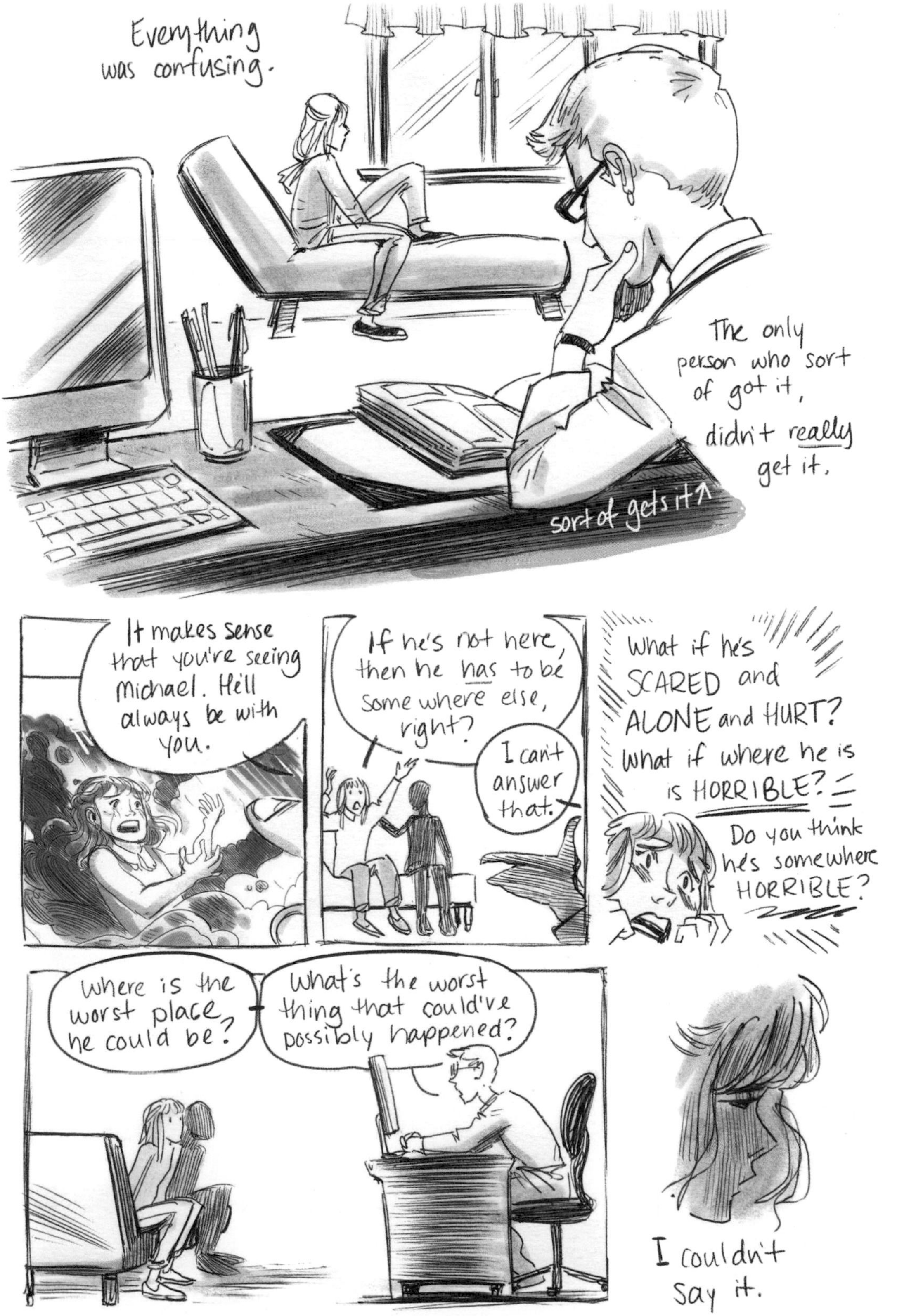
Everything was confusing.
The only person who sort of got it, didn't really get it.
sort of gets it ^
It makes sense that you're seeing Michael. He'll always be with you.
If he's not here, then he has to be some where else, right?
I can't answer that.
What if he's SCARED and ALONE and HURT? What if where he is is HORRIBLE?
Do you think he's somewhere HORRIBLE?
Where is the worst place he could be?
What's the worst thing that could've possibly happened?
I couldn't say it.

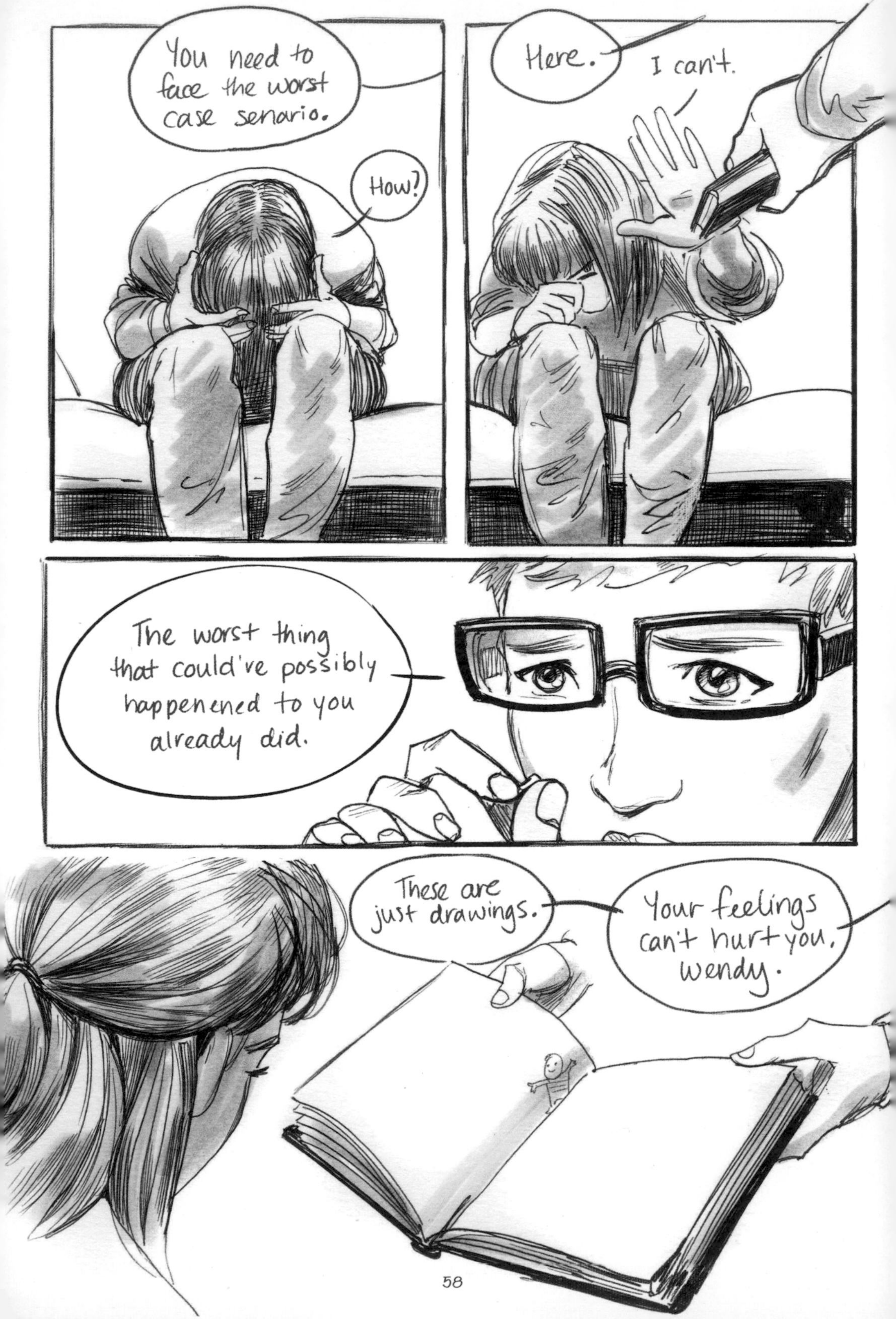
You need to face the worst case senario.
How?
Here.
I can't.
The worst thing that could've possibly happened to you already did.
These are just drawings.
Your feelings can't hurt you, Wendy.

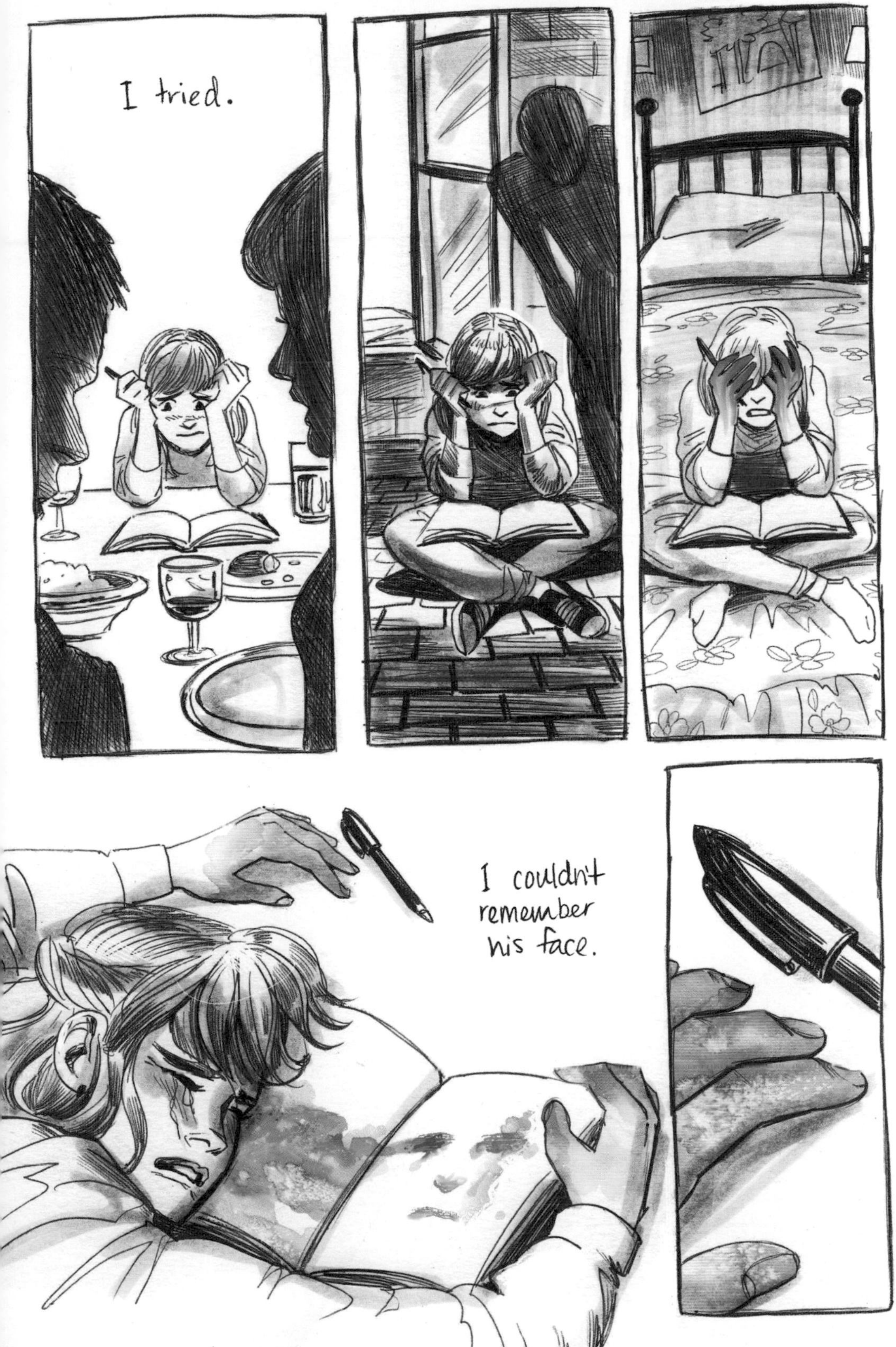
I tried.
I couldn't remember his face.

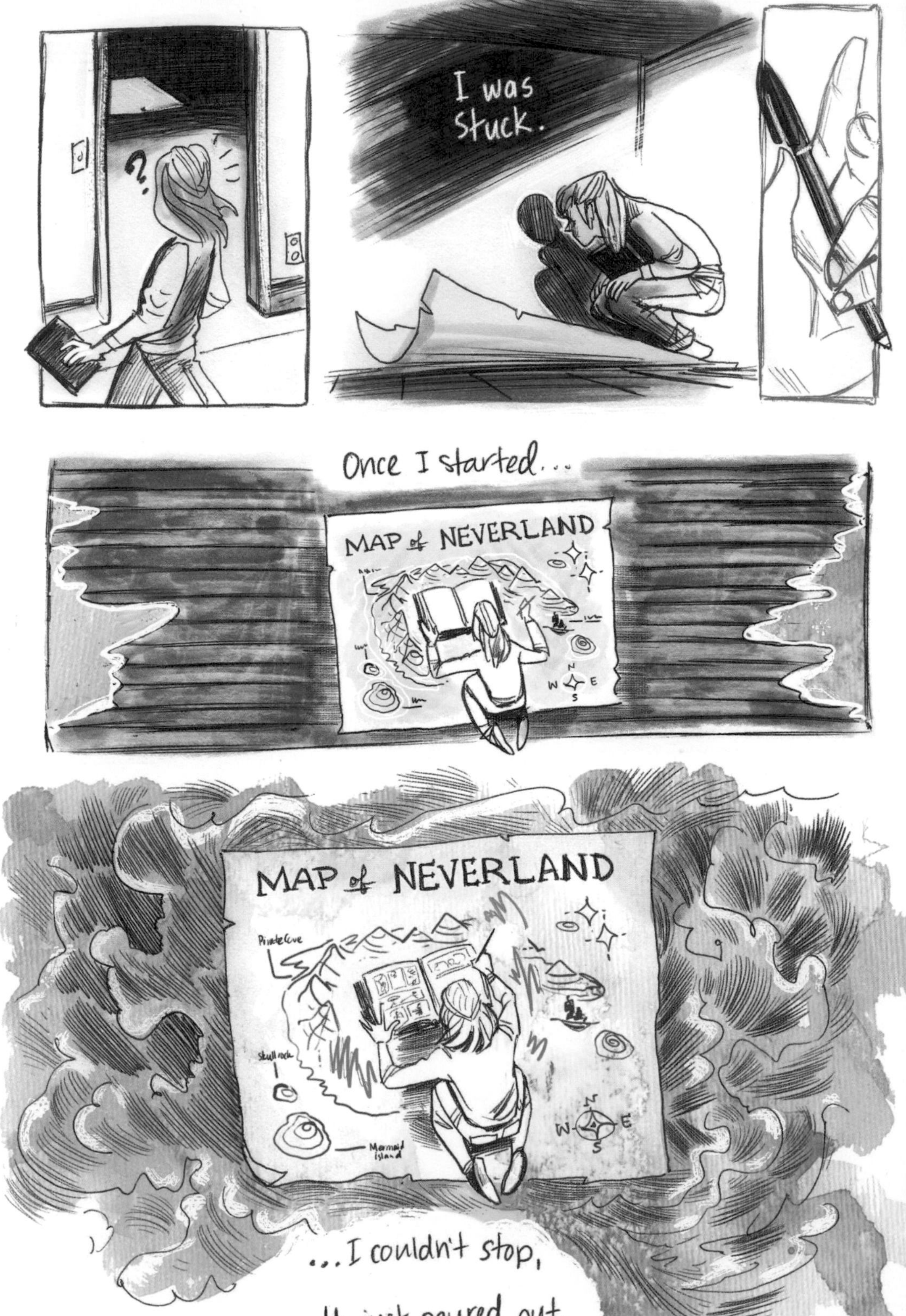
?
I was stuck.
Once I started...
MAP of NEVERLAND
N
W
E
S
MAP of NEVERLAND
Pirate Cove
Skull rock
Mermaid Island
N
W
E
S
...I couldn't stop,
It just poured out.

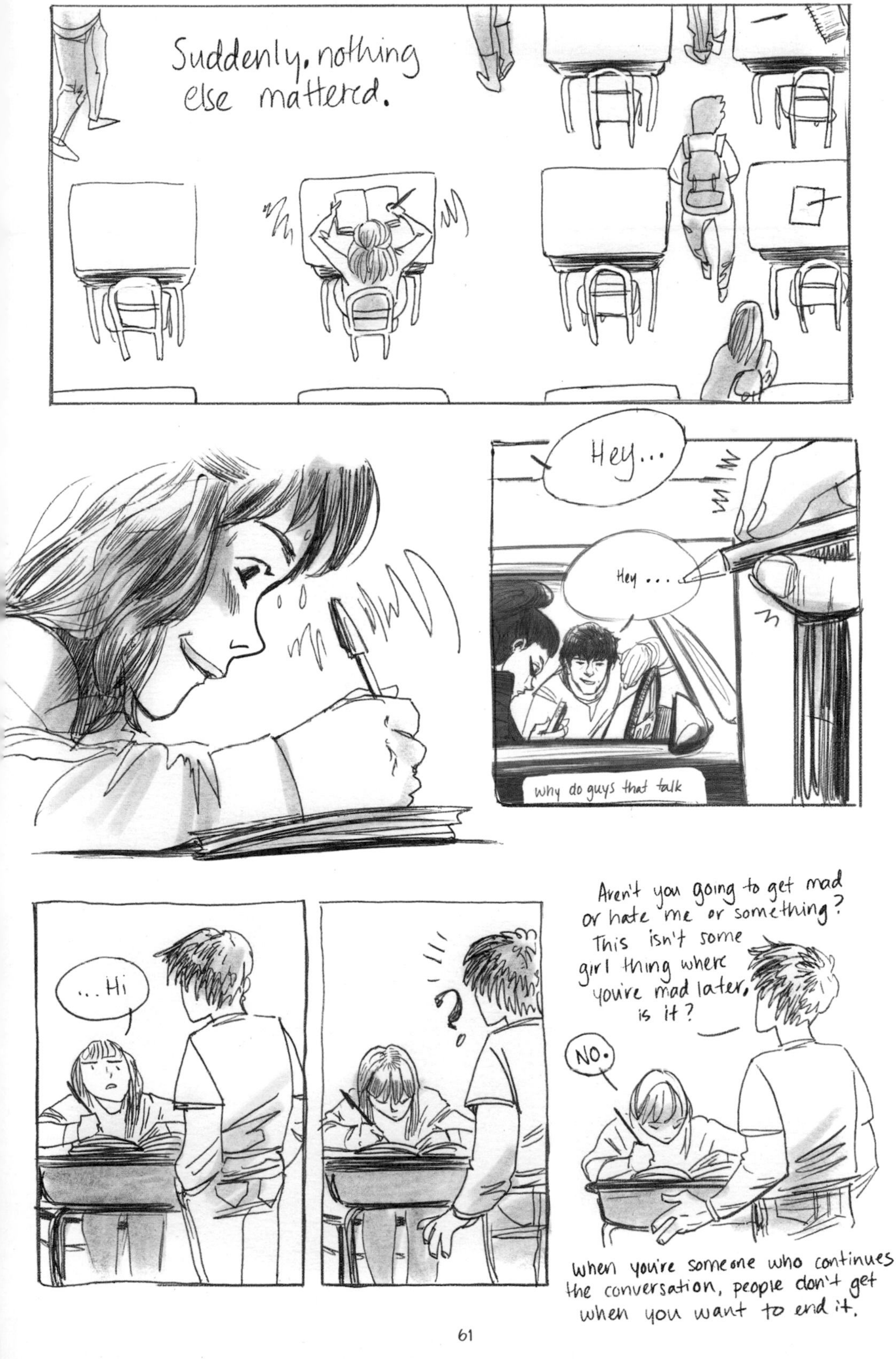
Suddenly, nothing else mattered.
Hey...
Hey...
why do guys that talk
...Hi
?
Aren't you going to get mad or hate me or something? This isn't some girl thing where you're mad later, is it?
NO.
when you're someone who continues the conversation, people don't get when you want to end it.

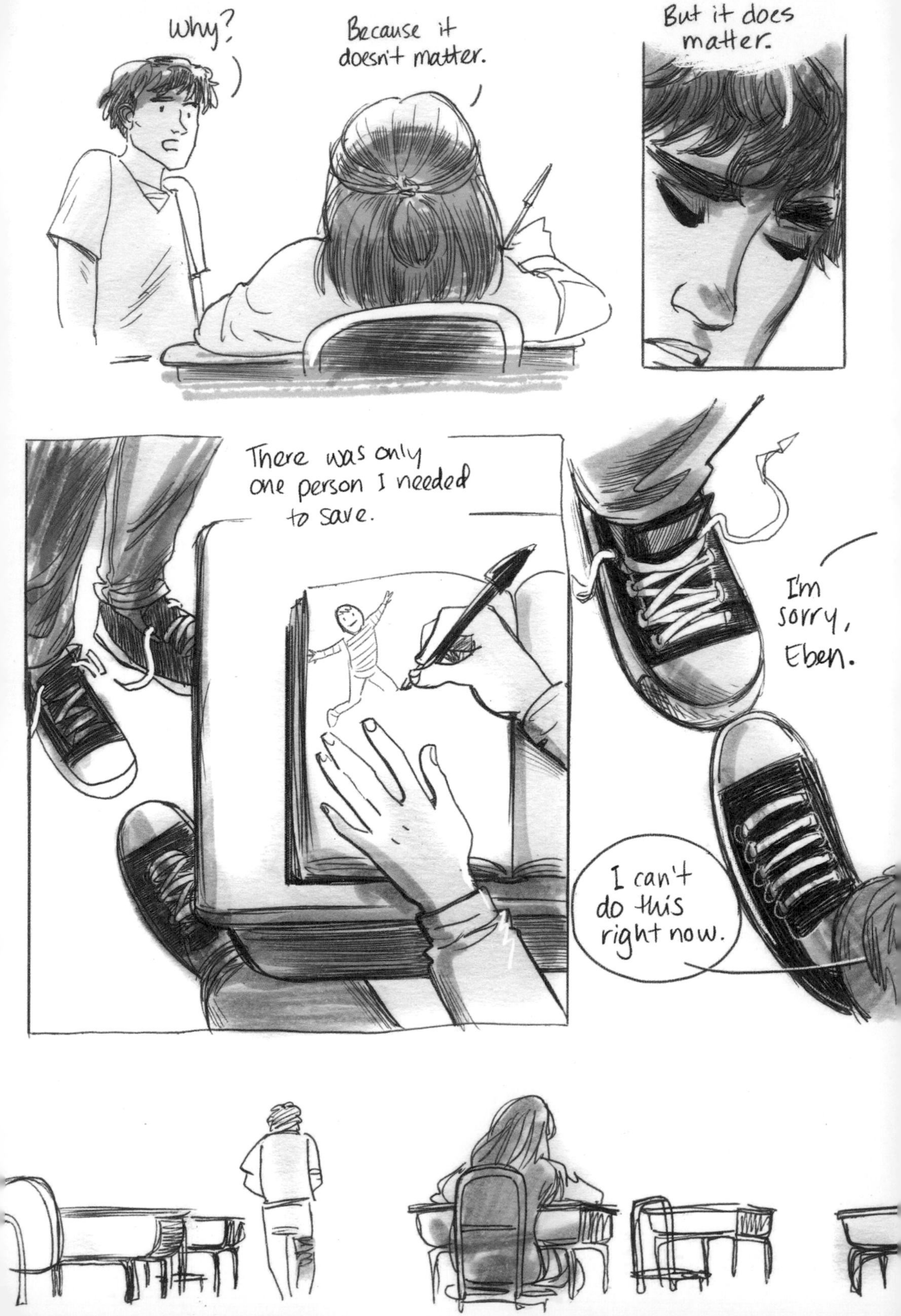
Why?
Because it doesn't matter.
But it does matter.
There was only one person I needed to save.
I'm sorry, Eben.
I can't do this right now.

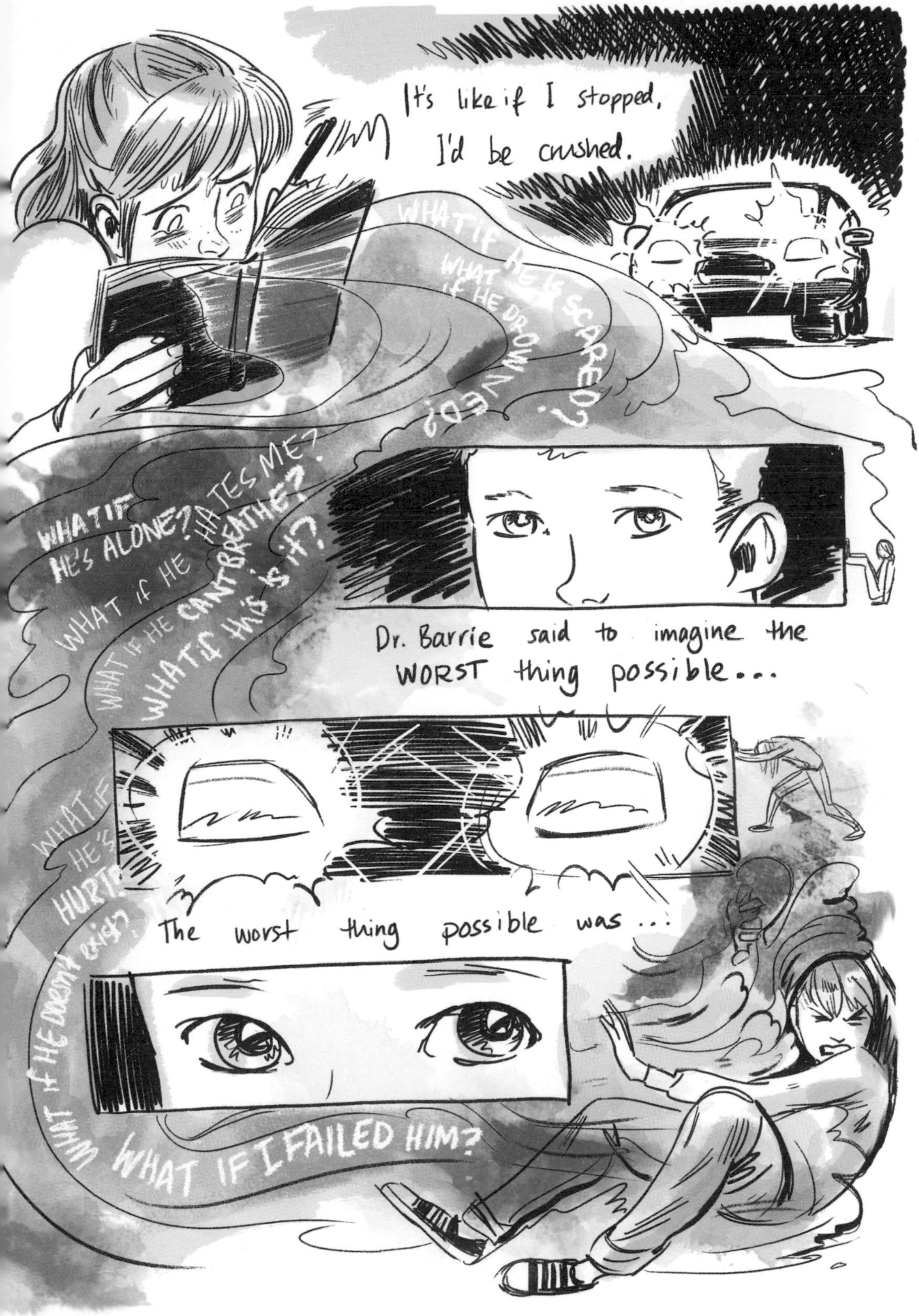
It's like if I stopped, I'd be crushed.
WHAT IF HE'S SCARED?
WHAT IF HE DROWNED?
WHAT IF HE'S ALONE?
WHAT IF HE HATES ME?
WHAT IF HE CANT BREATHE?
WHAT IF this is it?
Dr. Barrie said to imagine the WORST thing possible...
WHAT IF HE'S HURT?
WHAT IF HE DOESN'T exist?
The worst thing possible was...
WHAT IF I FAILED HIM?

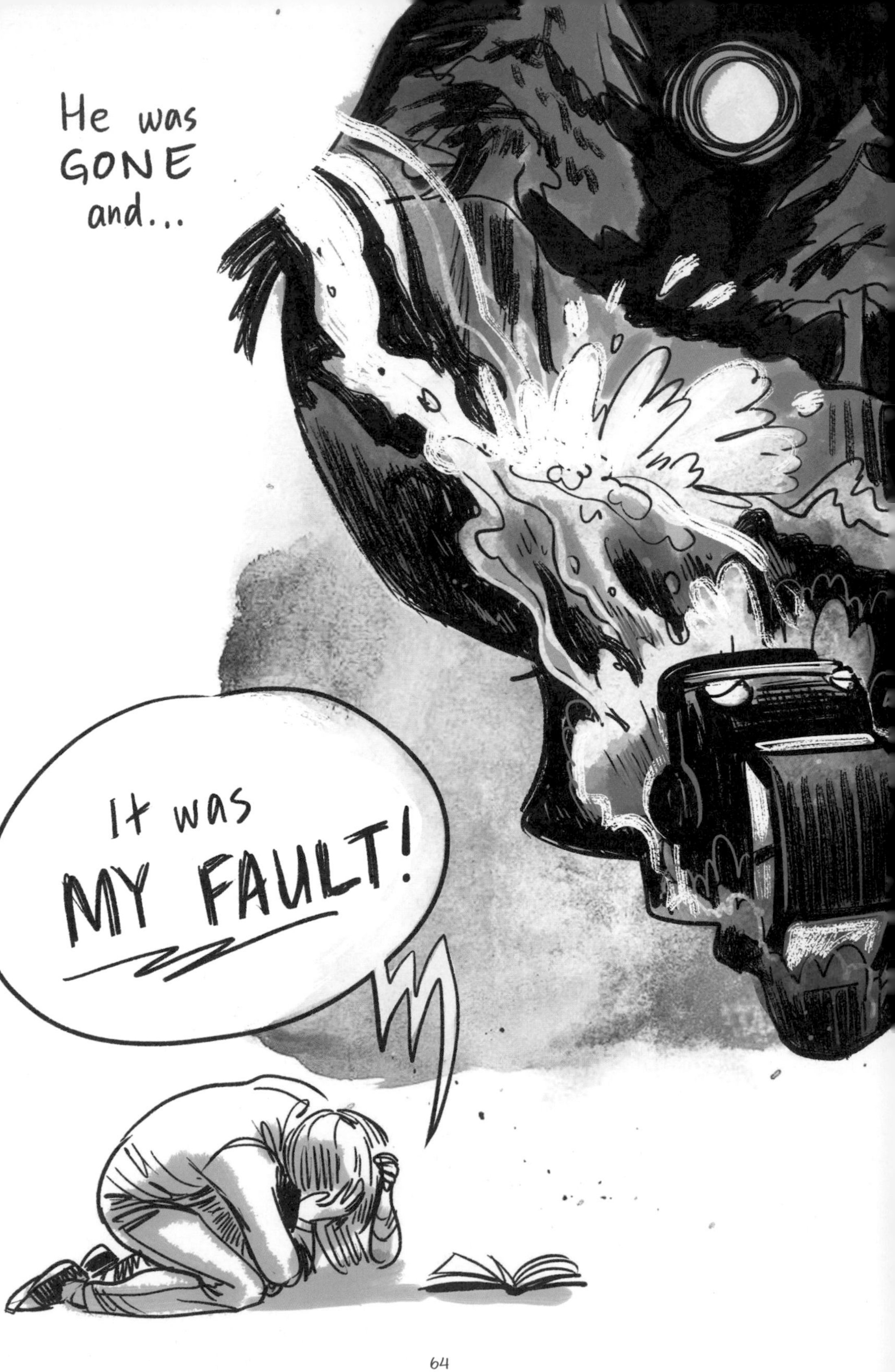
He was GONE and...
It was MY FAULT!

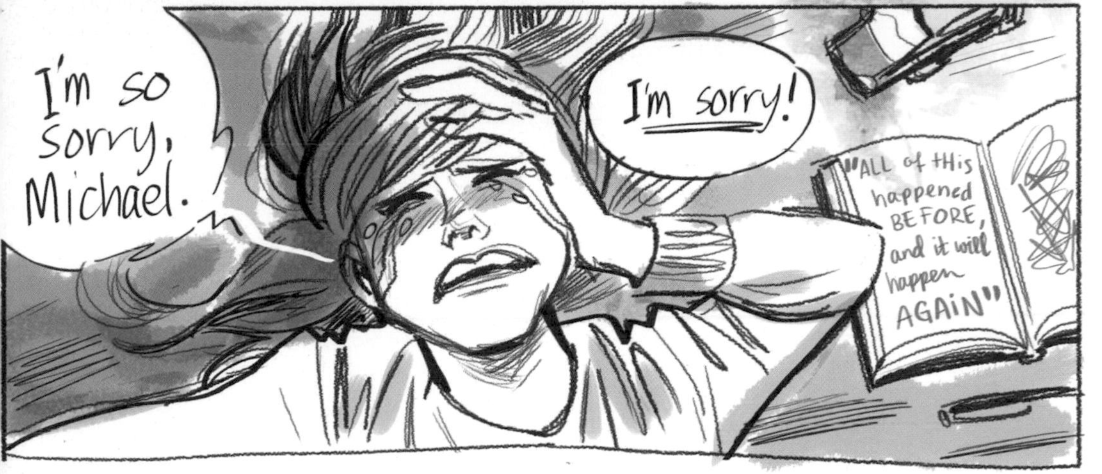
I'm so sorry, Michael.
I'm sorry!
"ALL of tHis happened BEFORE, and it will happen AGAIN"

He was gone. And I was the only one that could face it.

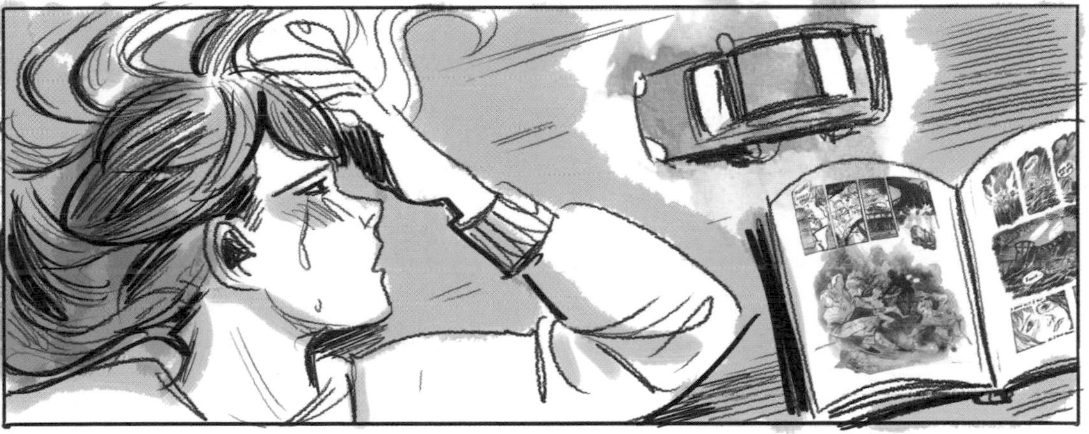

It was a sign.

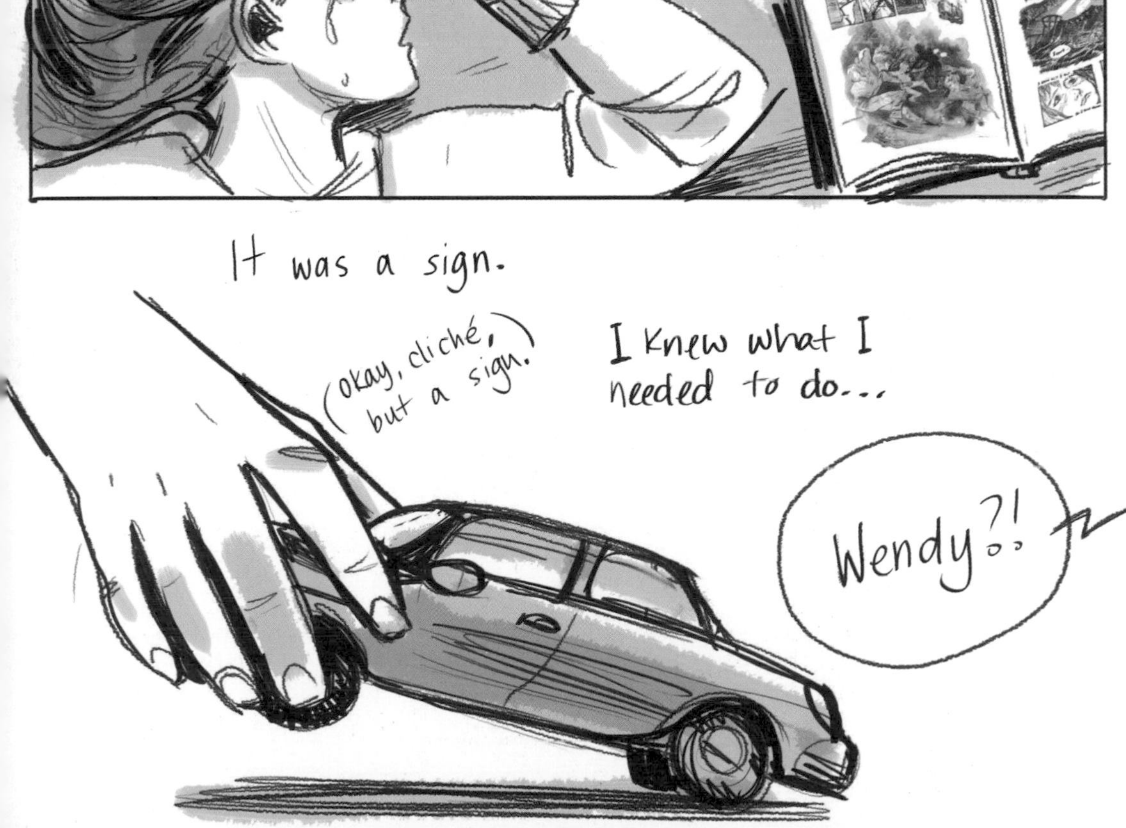
(okay, cliché, but a sign.)
I knew what I needed to do...
Wendy?!

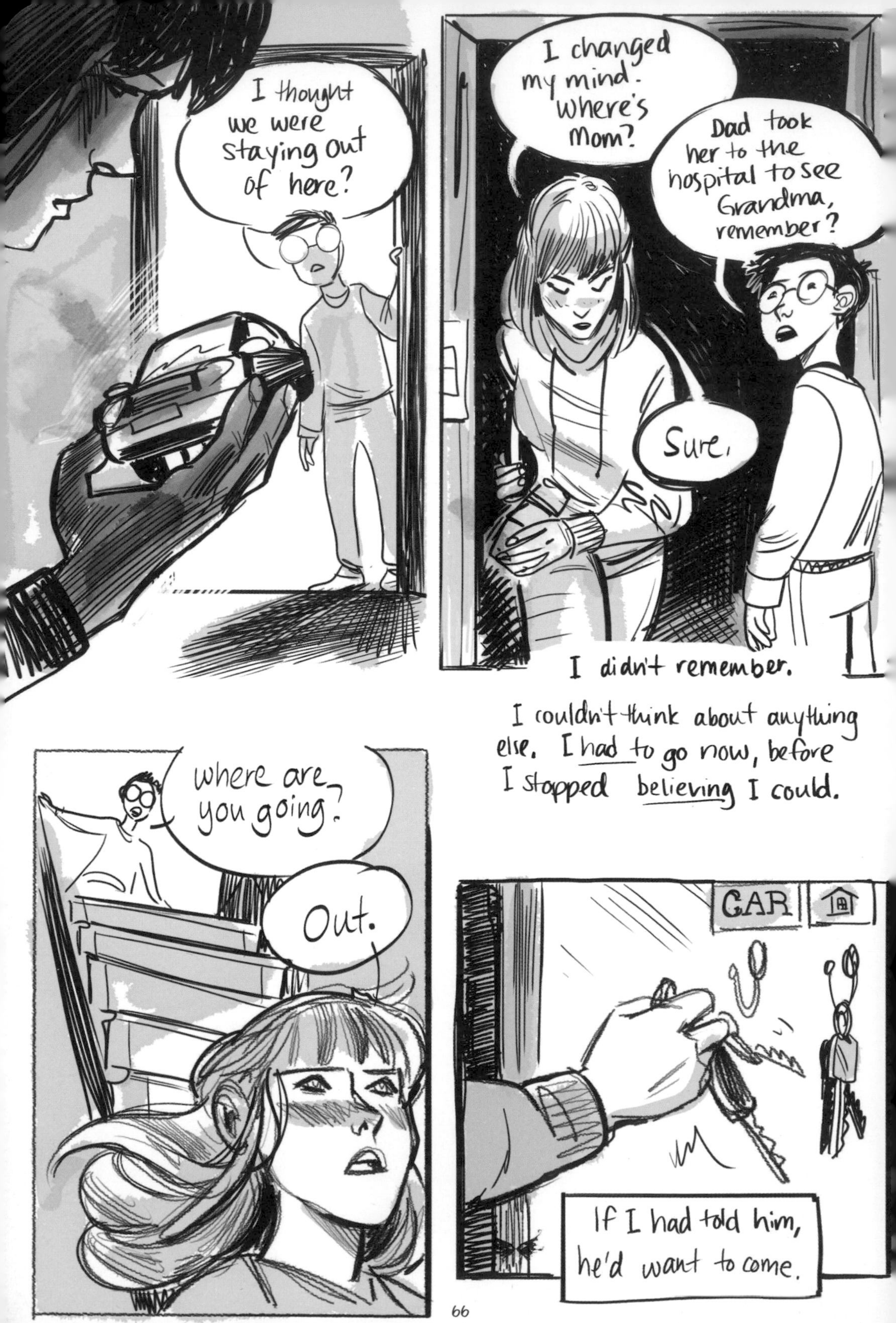
I thought we were staying out of here?
I changed my mind. Where's Mom?
Dad took her to the hospital to see Grandma, remember?
Sure.
I didn't remember.
I couldn't think about anything else. I had to go now, before I stopped believing I could.
Where are you going?
Out.
CAR
If I had told him, he'd want to come.

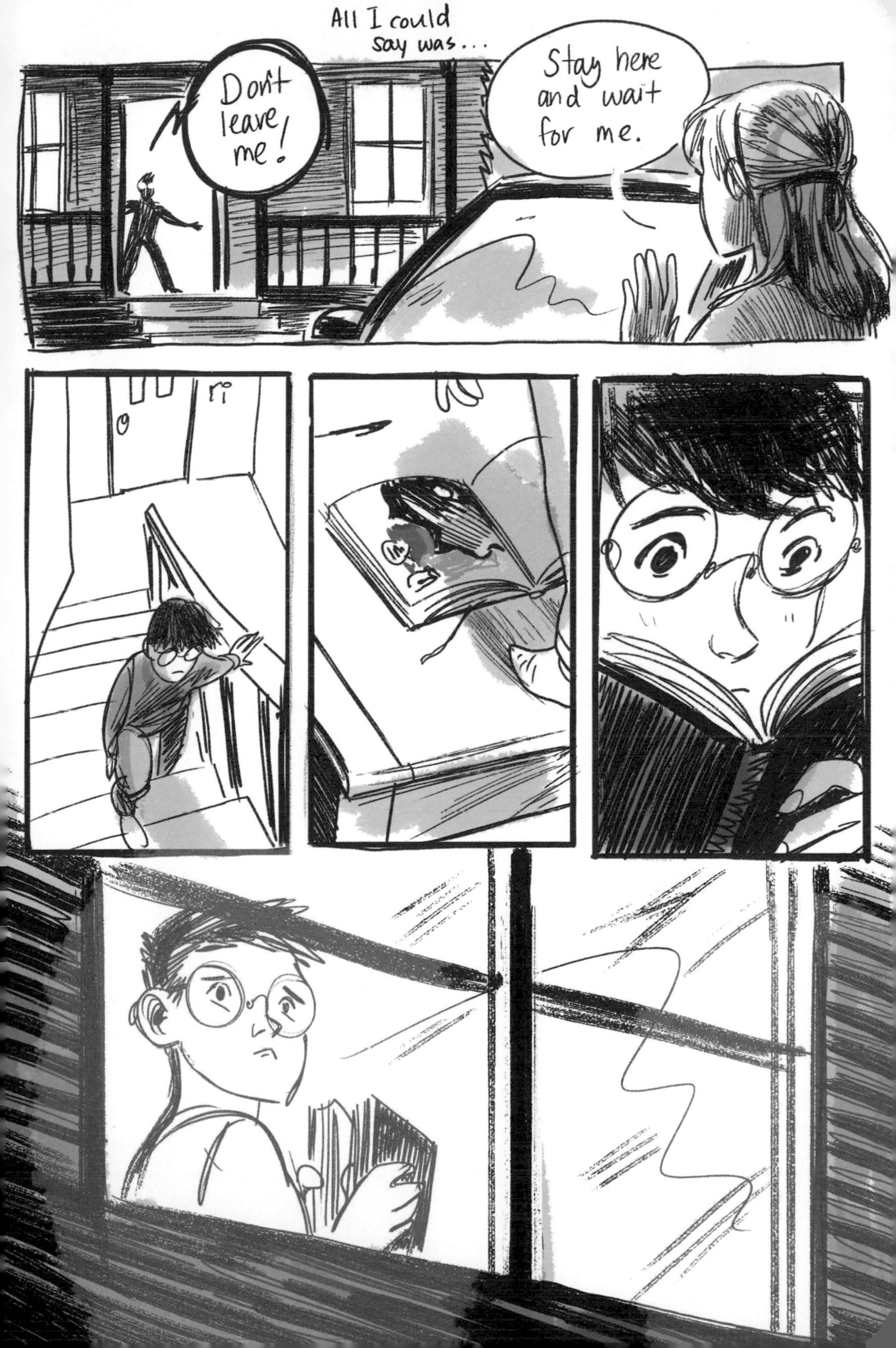
All I could say was...
Don't leave me!
Stay here and wait for me.

for to have faith is to have wings

This may seem like I have a death wish — I don't, I swear...

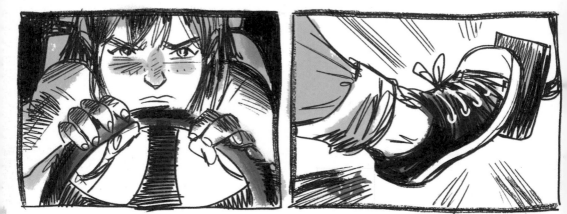

I BELIEVED.

I had to believe in something.

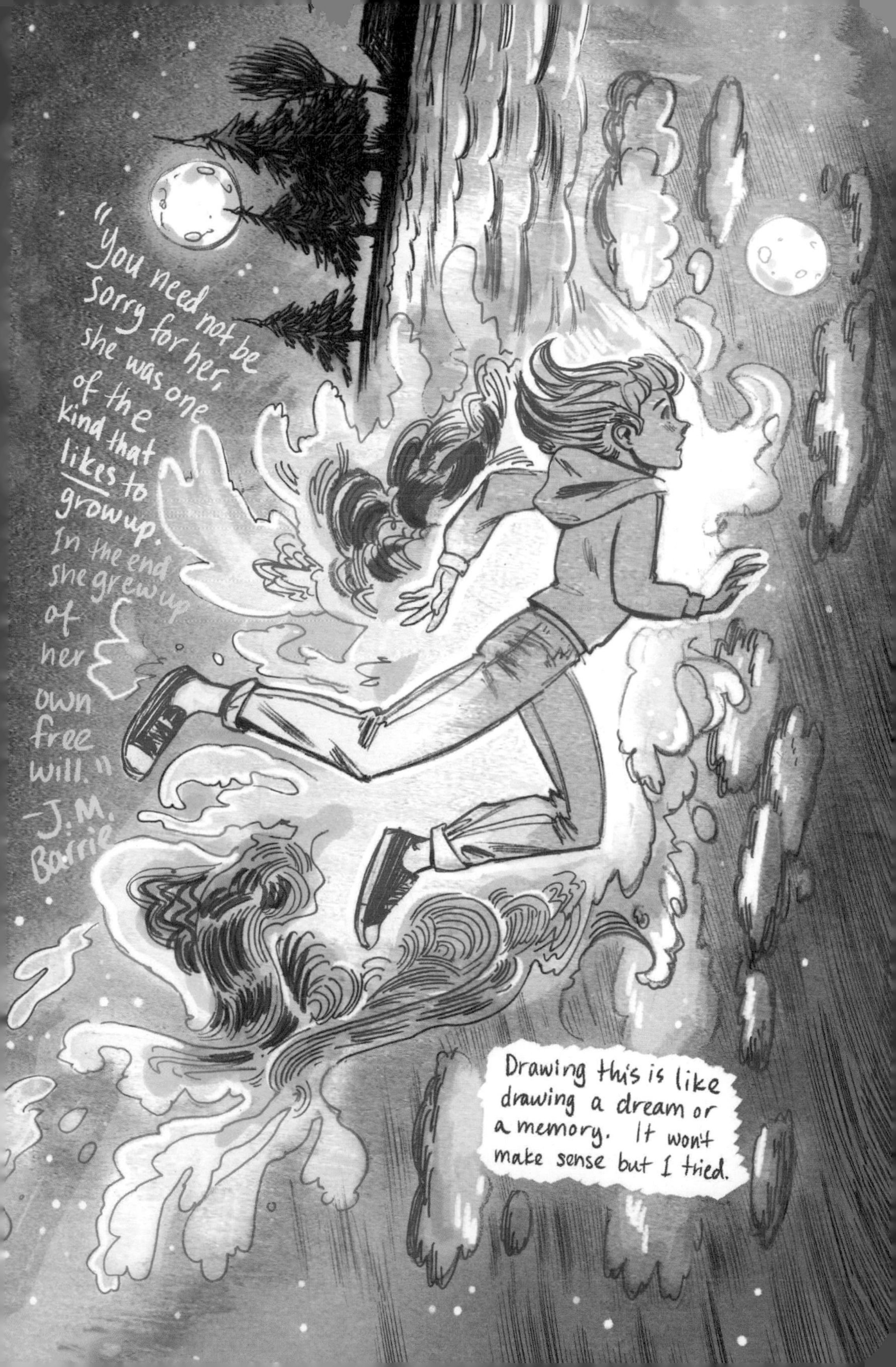
"You need not be sorry for her, she was one of the kind that likes to grow up. In the end she grew up of her own free will." -J.M. Barrie
Drawing this is like drawing a dream or a memory. It won't make sense but I tried.

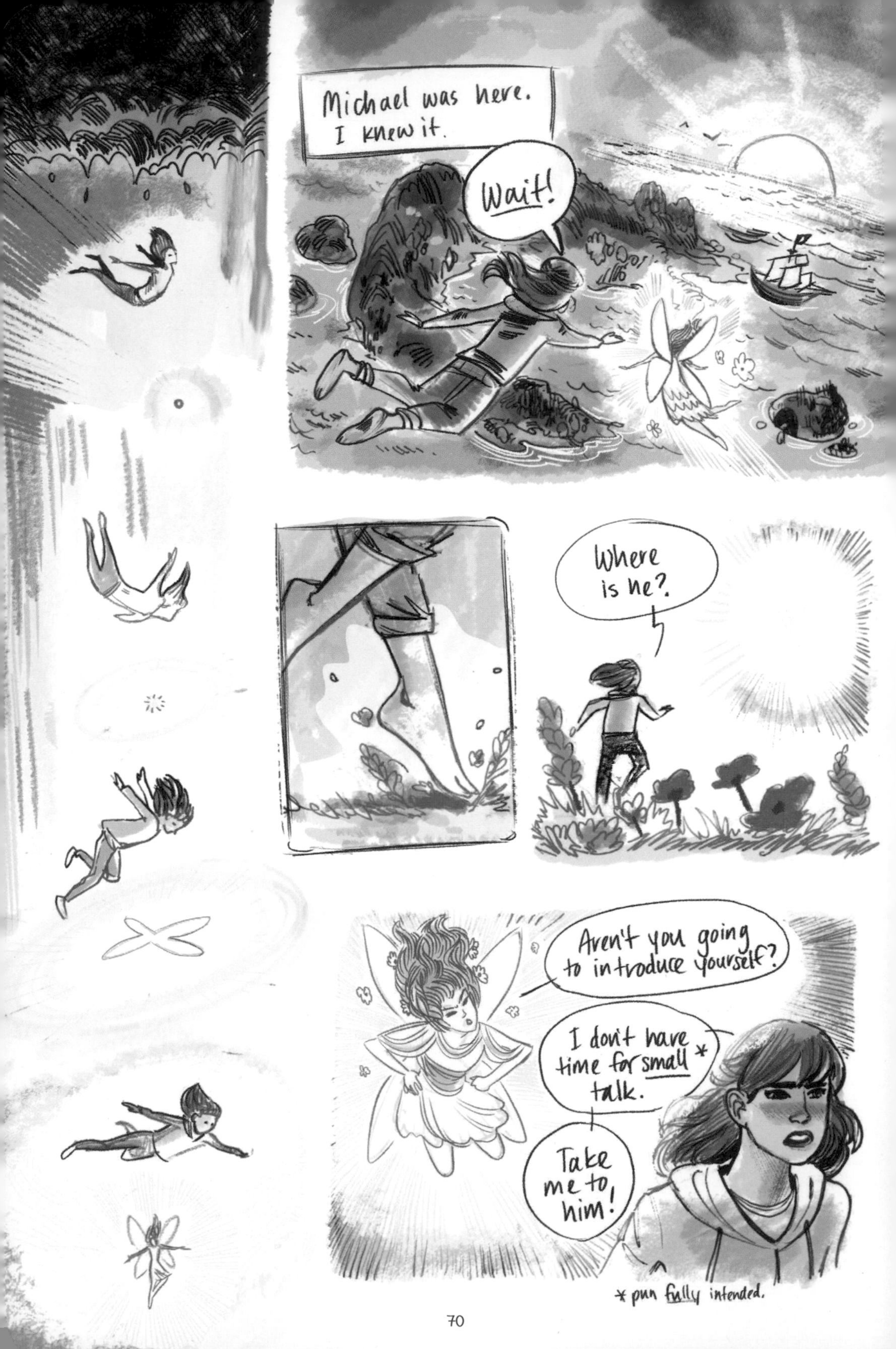

Michael was here. I knew it.
Wait!
Where is he?
Aren't you going to introduce yourself?
I don't have time for small* talk.
Take me to him!
*pun fully intended.

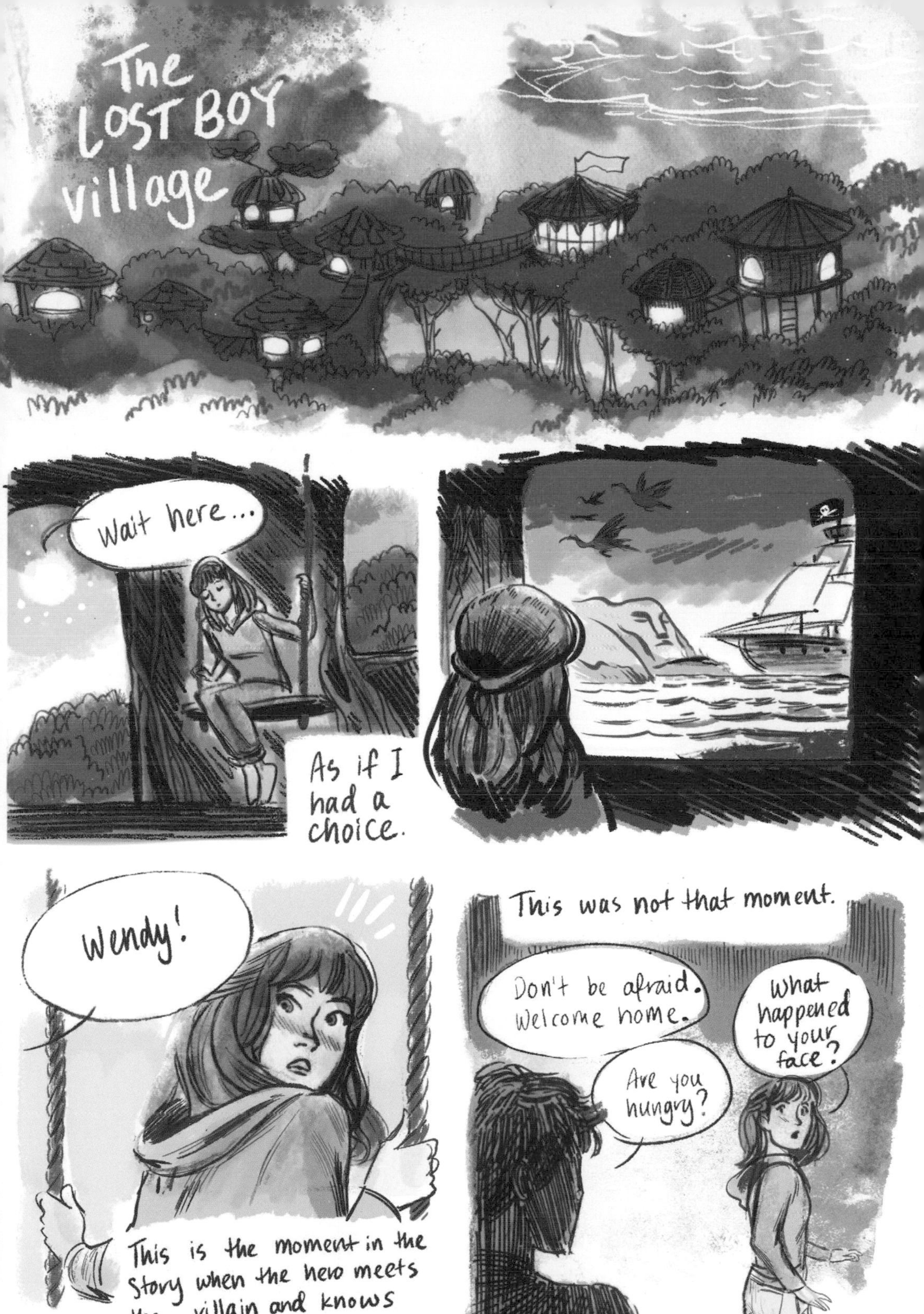

The LOST BOY village
Wait here...
As if I had a choice.
Wendy!
This is the moment in the story when the hero meets the villain and knows exactly what to say...
This was not that moment.
Don't be afraid. Welcome home.
Are you hungry?
What happened to your face?

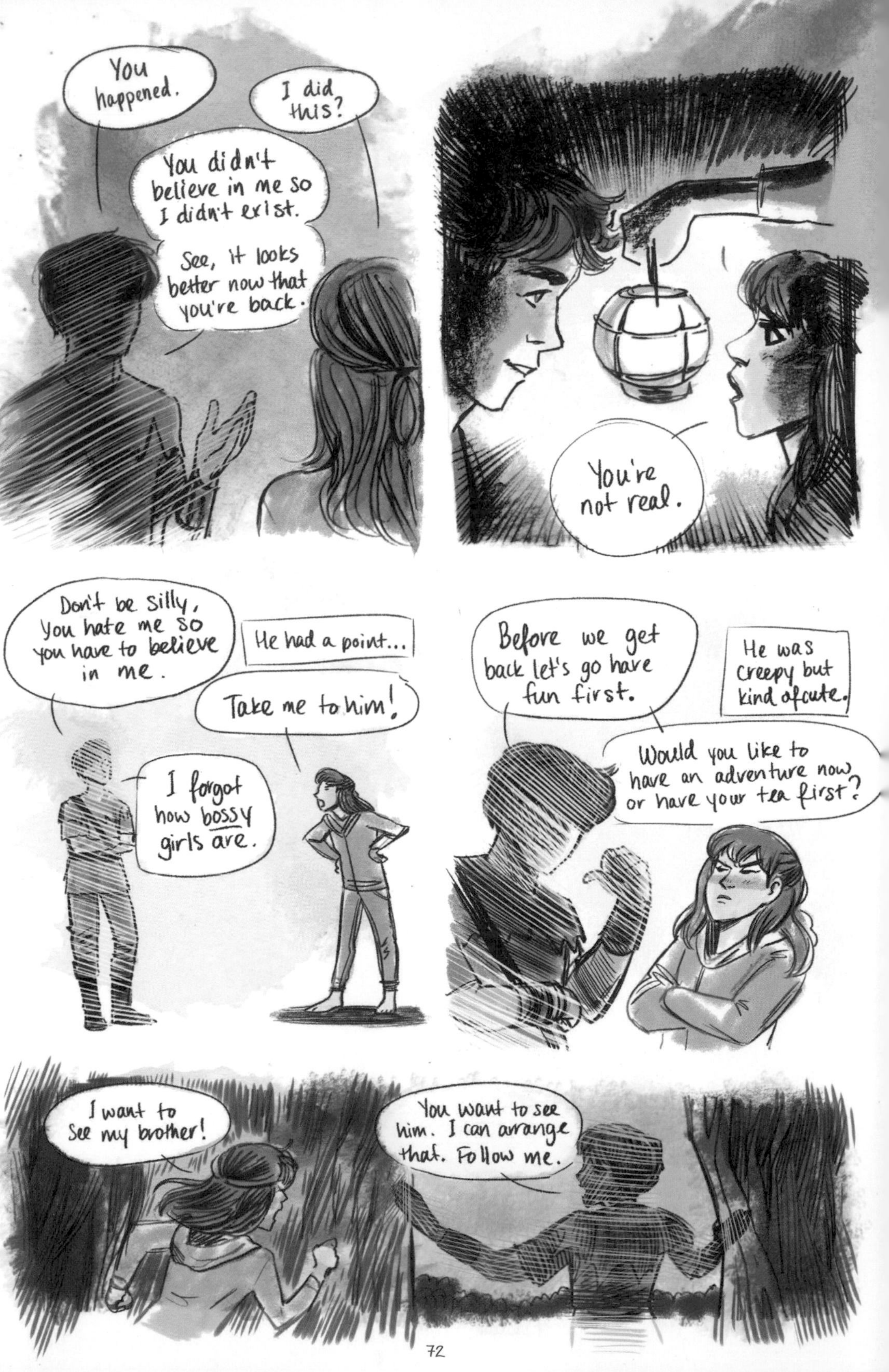
You happened.
I did this?
You didn't believe in me so I didn't exist.
See, it looks better now that you're back.
You're not real.
Don't be silly, You hate me so you have to believe in me.
He had a point...
Take me to him!
I forgot how bossy girls are.
Before we get back let's go have fun first.
He was creepy but kind of cute.
Would you like to have an adventure now or have your tea first?
I want to see my brother!
You want to see him. I can arrange that. Follow me.

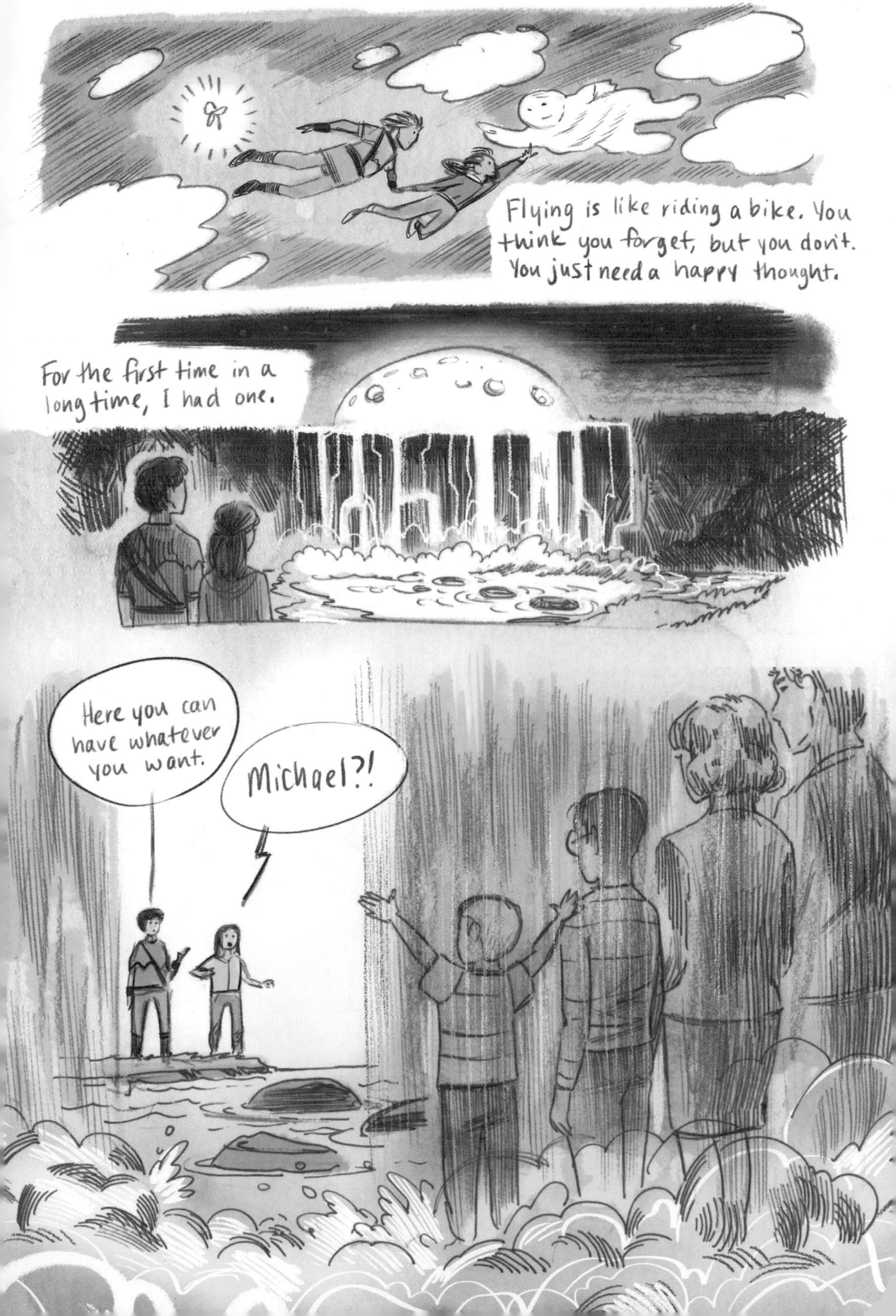
Flying is like riding a bike. You think you forget, but you don't. You just need a happy thought.
For the first time in a long time, I had one.
Here you can have whatever you want.
Michael?!

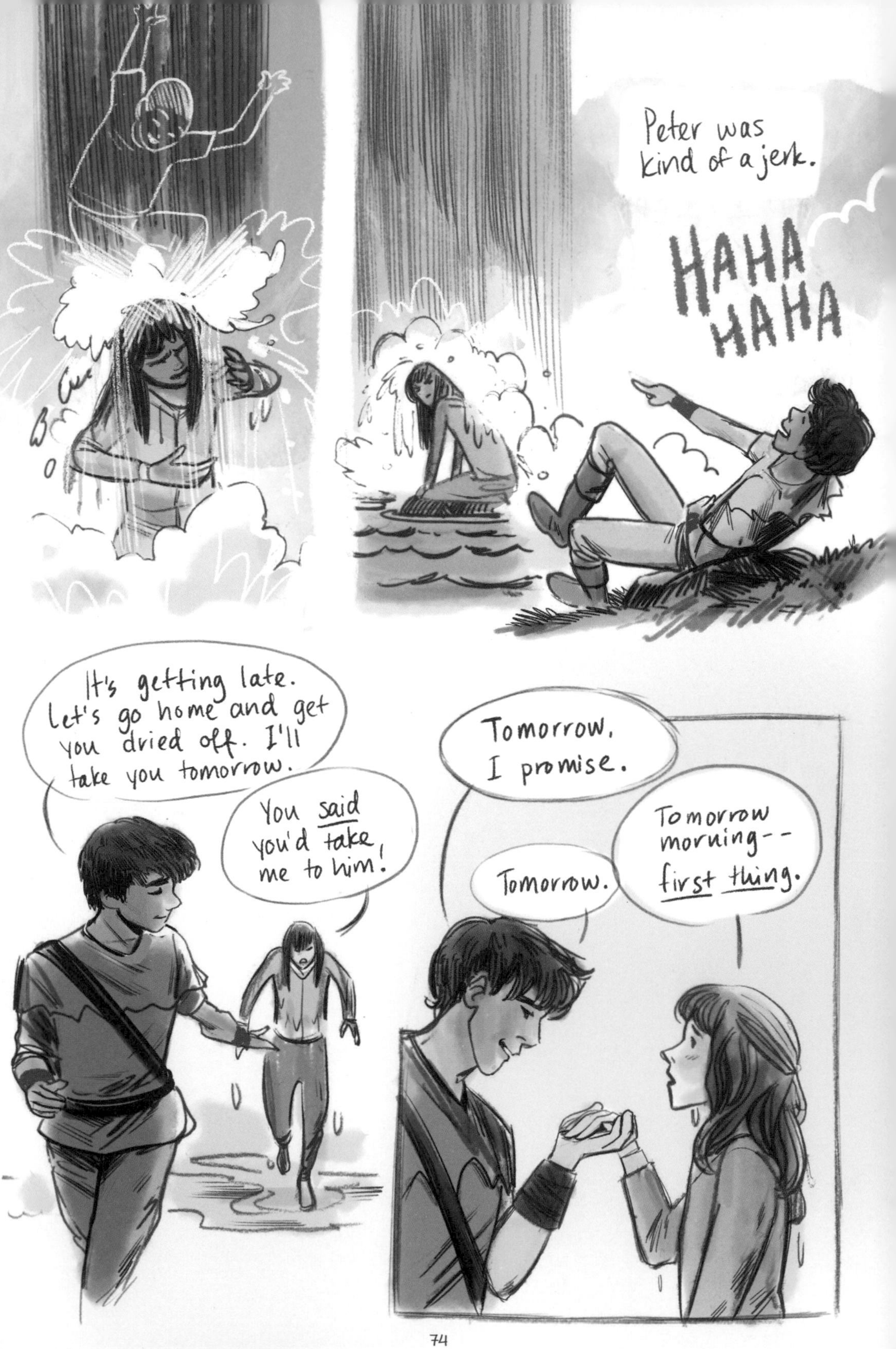
Peter was kind of a jerk.
HAHA HAHA
It's getting late. Let's go home and get you dried off. I'll take you tomorrow.
You said you'd take me to him!
Tomorrow, I promise.
Tomorrow.
Tomorrow morning-- first thing.

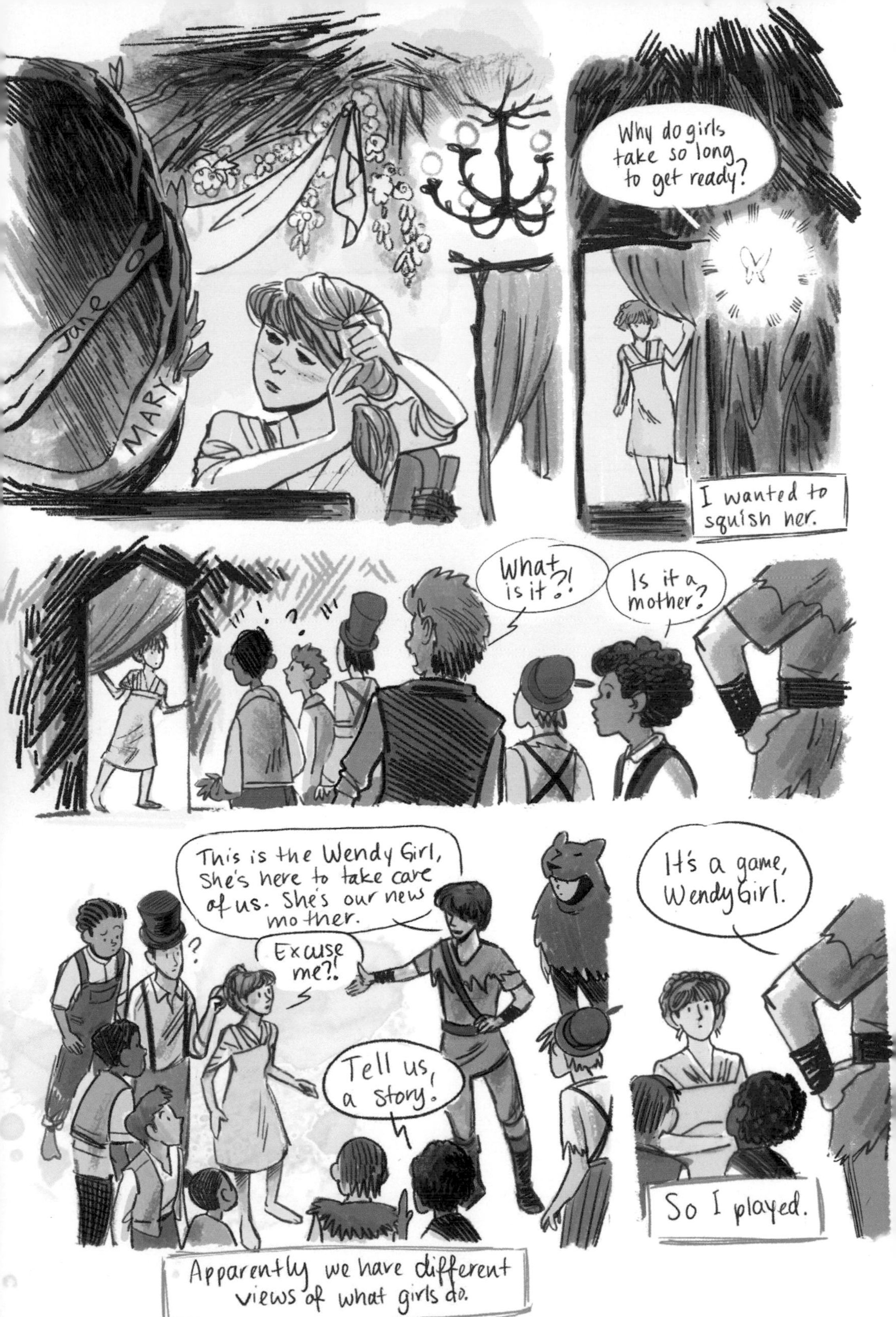
Jane
MARY
Why do girls take so long to get ready?
I wanted to squish her.
What is it?!
Is it a mother?
This is the Wendy Girl, she's here to take care of us. She's our new mother.
Excuse me?!
Tell us, a story!
Apparently we have different views of what girls do.
It's a game, Wendy Girl.
So I played.

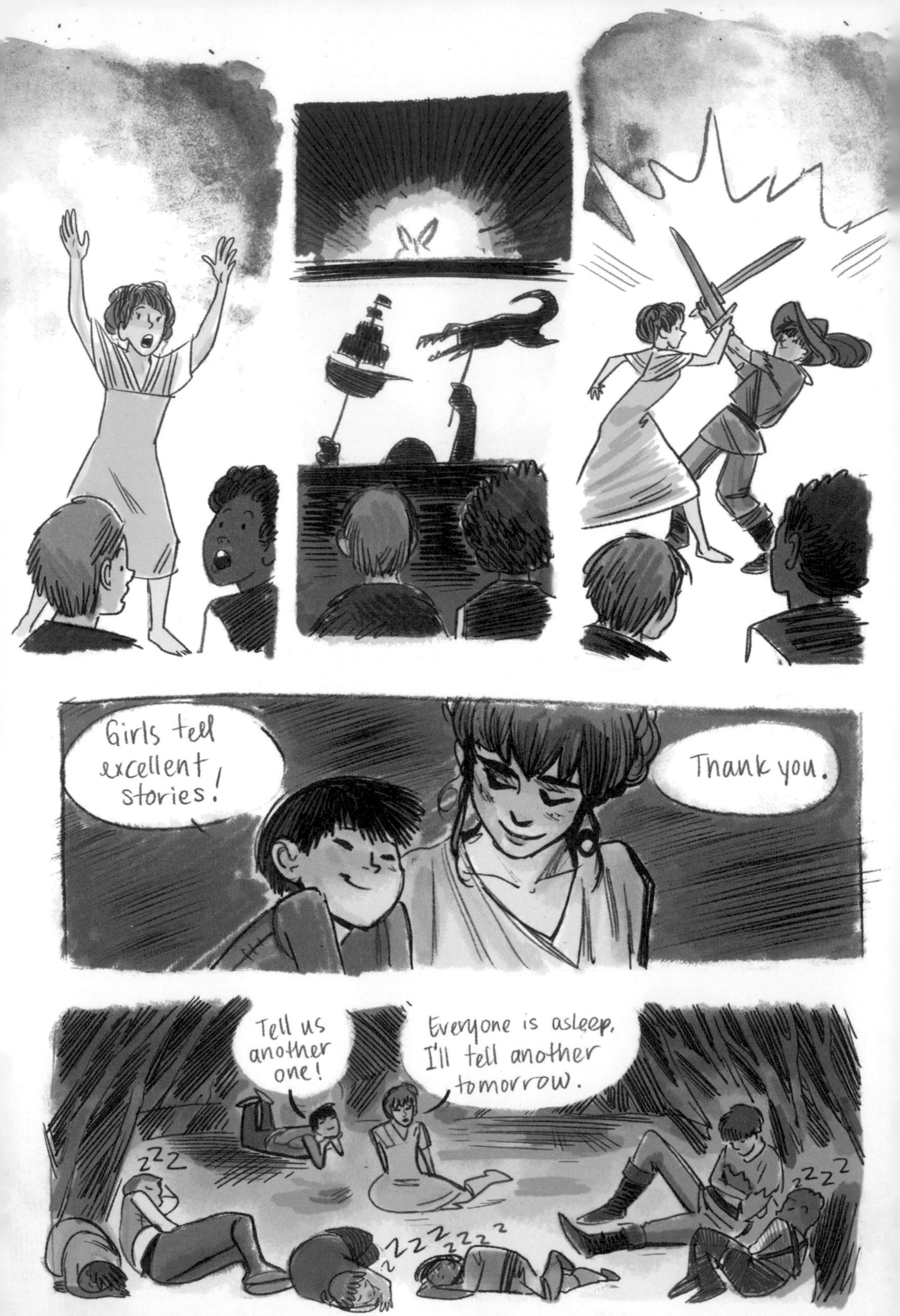
Girls tell excellent stories!
Thank you.
Tell us another one!
Everyone is asleep. I'll tell another tomorrow.
ZZZ
ZZZZZZZ
ZZZZ

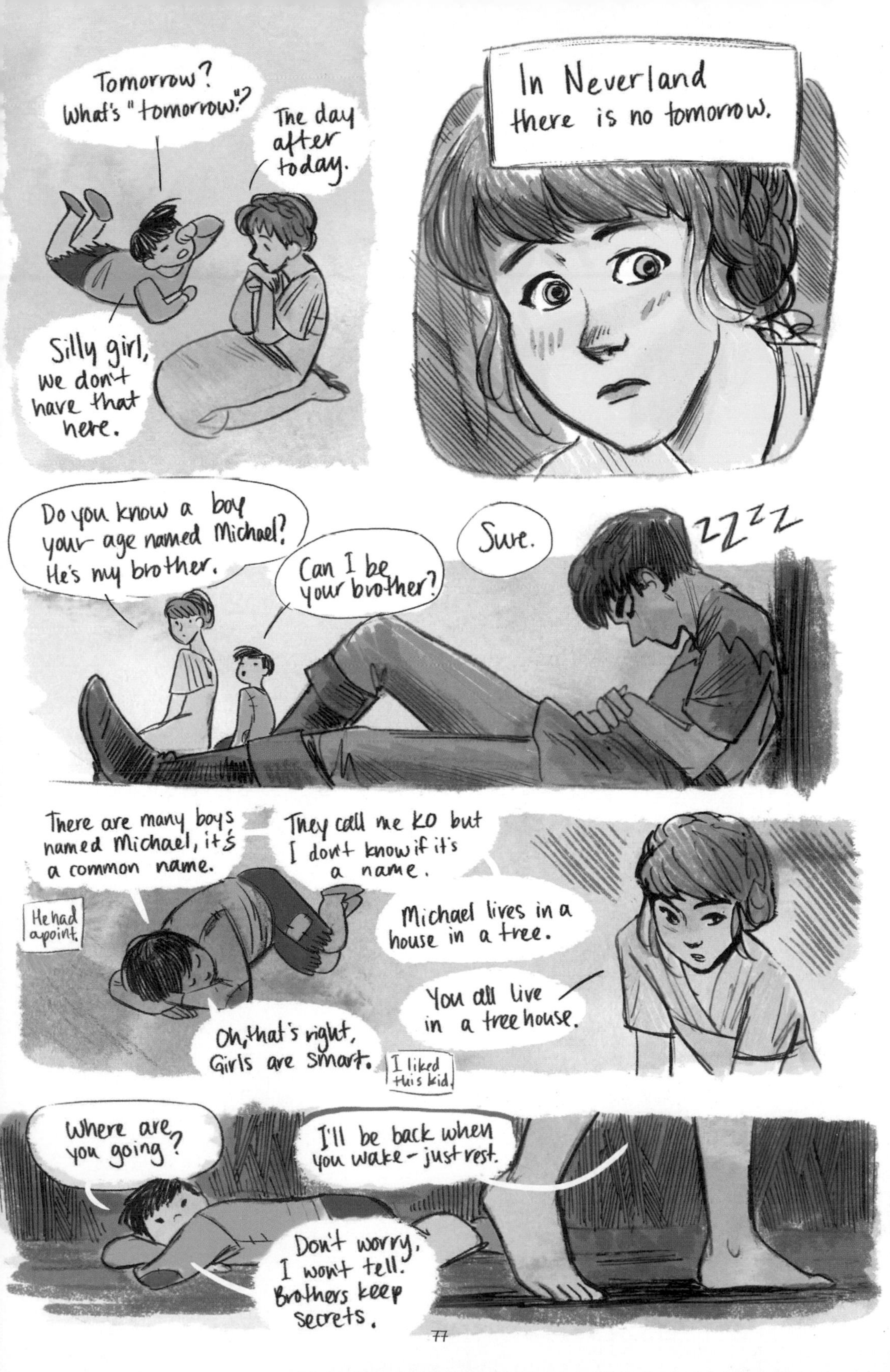
Tomorrow? What's "tomorrow"?
The day after today.
Silly girl, we don't have that here.
In Neverland there is no tomorrow.
Do you know a boy your age named Michael? He's my brother.
Can I be your brother?
Sure.
ZZZZ
There are many boys named Michael, it's a common name.
They call me KO but I don't know if it's a name.
He had a point.
Michael lives in a house in a tree.
You all live in a tree house.
Oh, that's right, Girls are smart.
I liked this kid.
Where are you going?
I'll be back when you wake - just rest.
Don't worry, I won't tell. Brothers keep secrets.

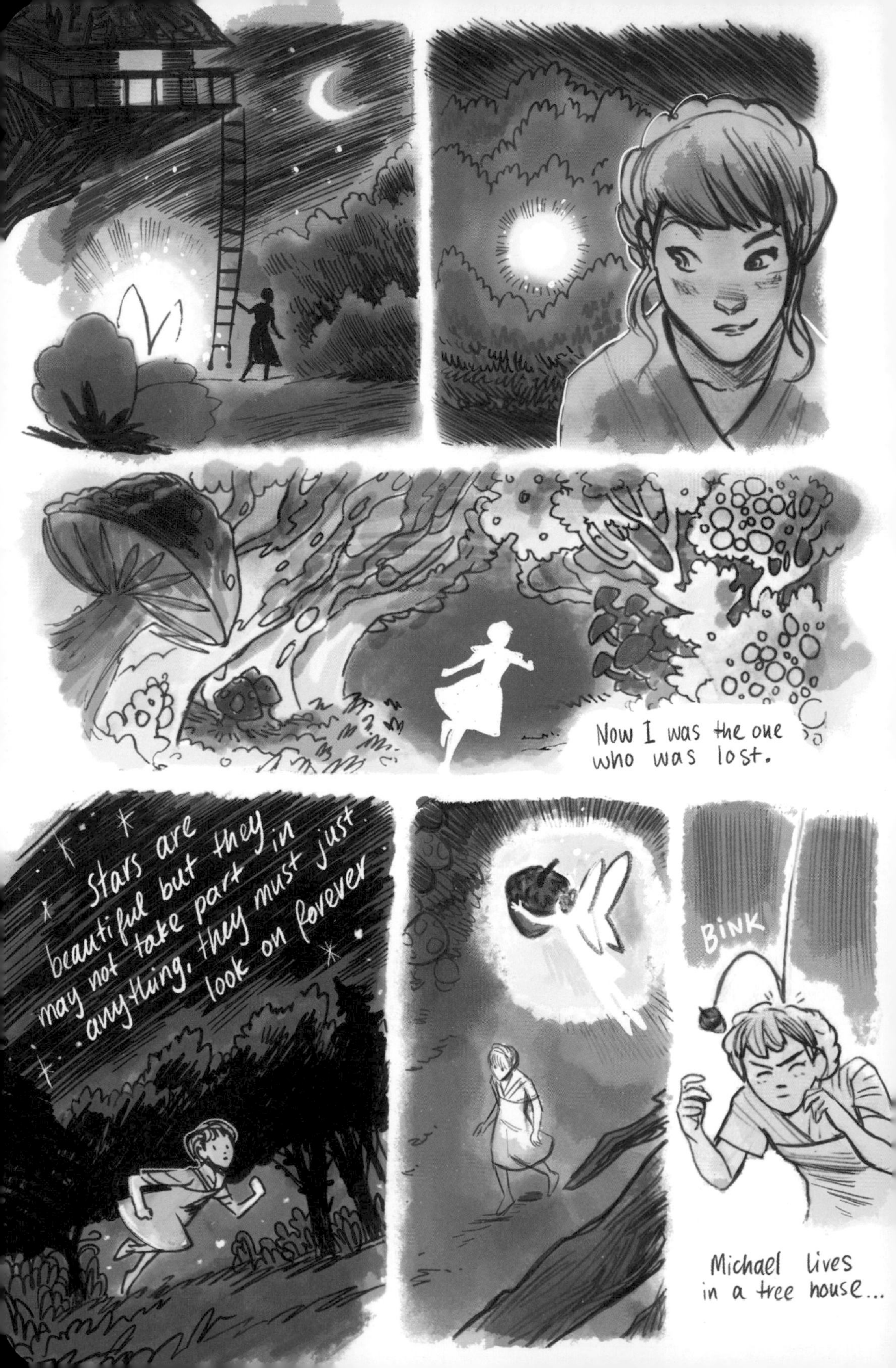
Now I was the one who was lost.
Stars are beautiful but they may not take part in anything, they must just look on forever
BINK
Michael lives in a tree house...

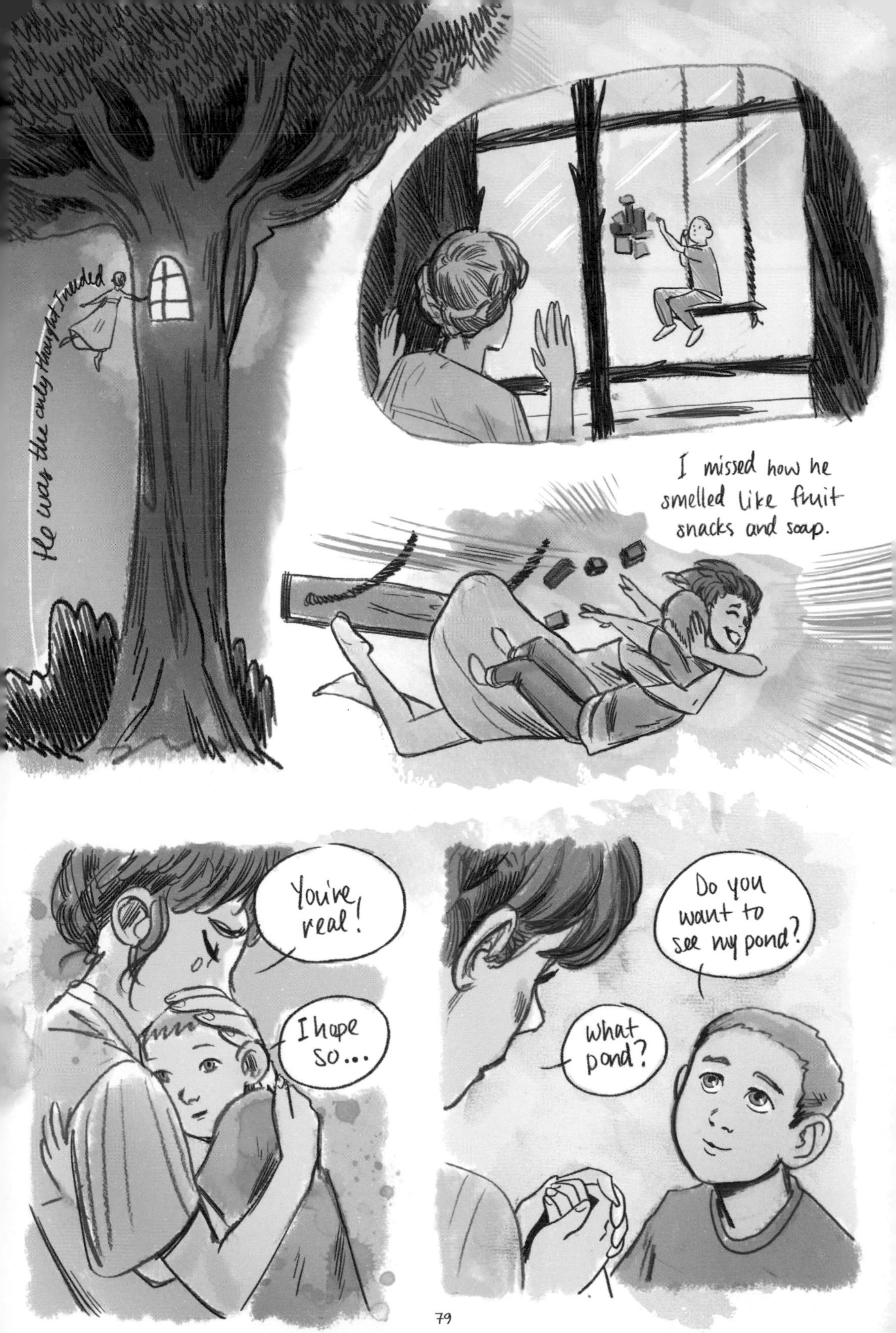
He was the only thought I needed
I missed how he smelled like fruit snacks and soap.
You're real!
I hope so...
Do you want to see my pond?
What pond?

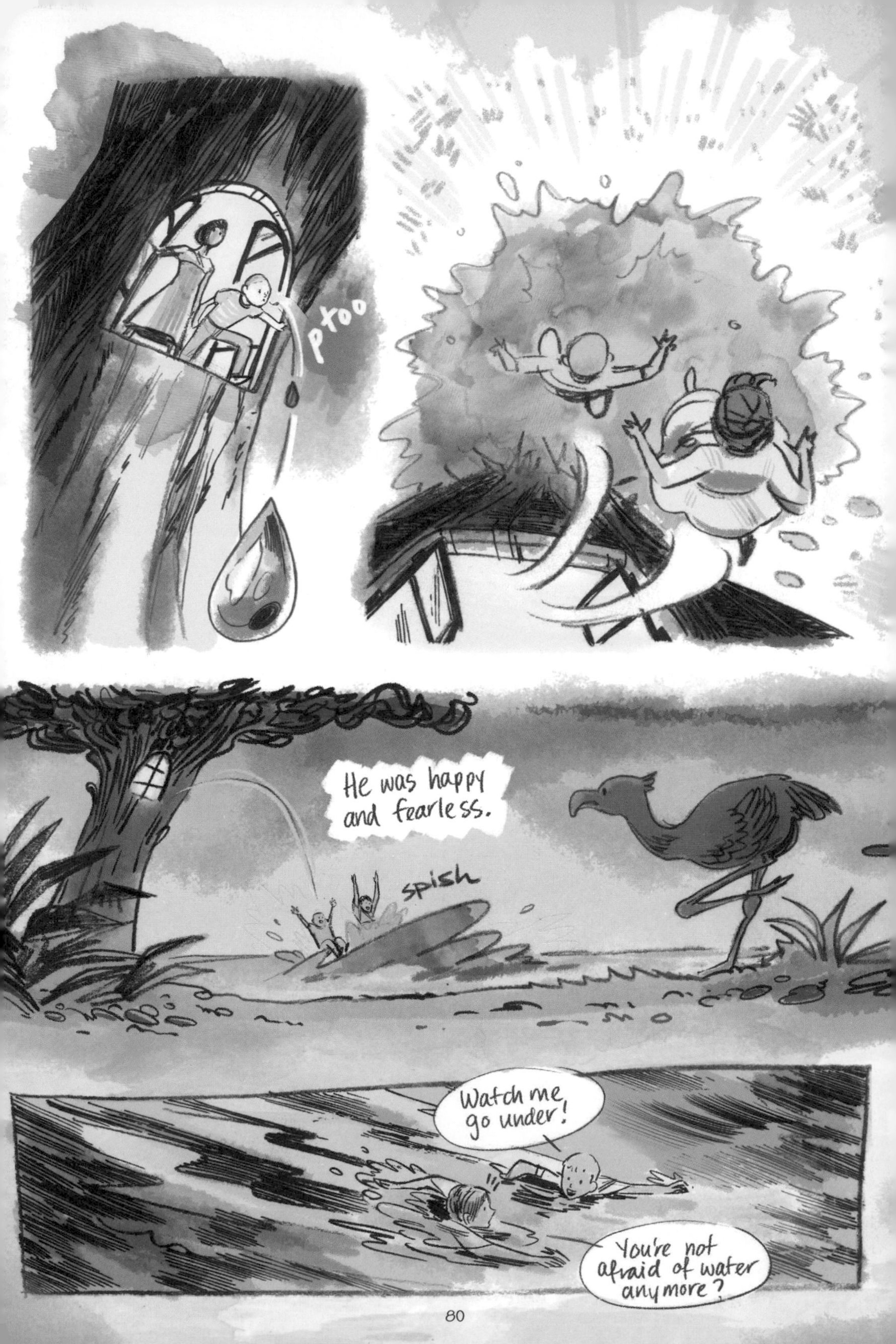
ptoo
He was happy and fearless.
spish
Watch me go under!
You're not afraid of water anymore?

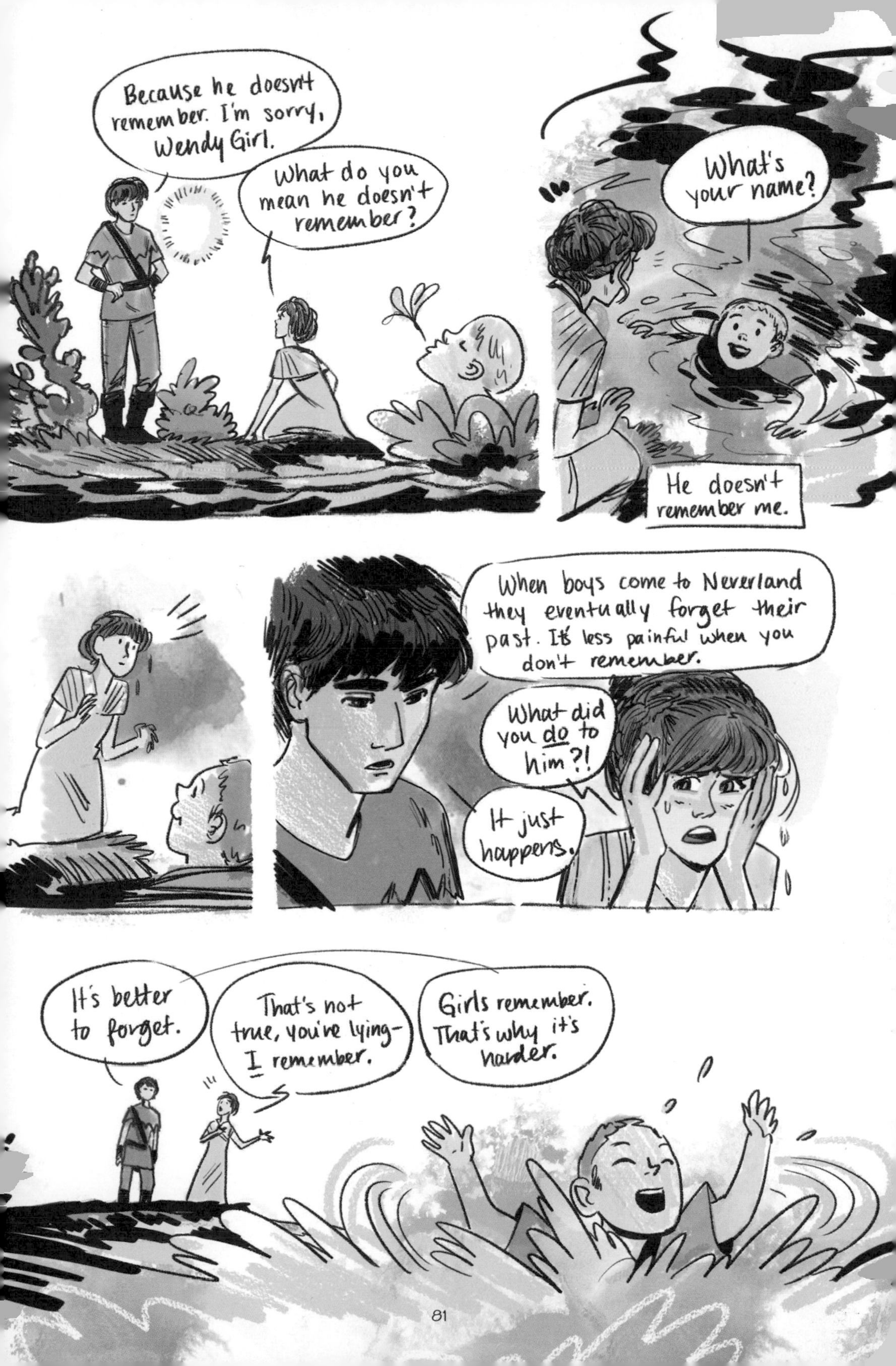

Because he doesn't remember. I'm sorry, Wendy Girl.
What do you mean he doesn't remember?
What's your name?
He doesn't remember me.
When boys come to Neverland they eventually forget their past. It's less painful when you don't remember.
What did you do to him?!
It just happens.
It's better to forget.
That's not true, you're lying- I remember.
Girls remember. That's why it's harder.

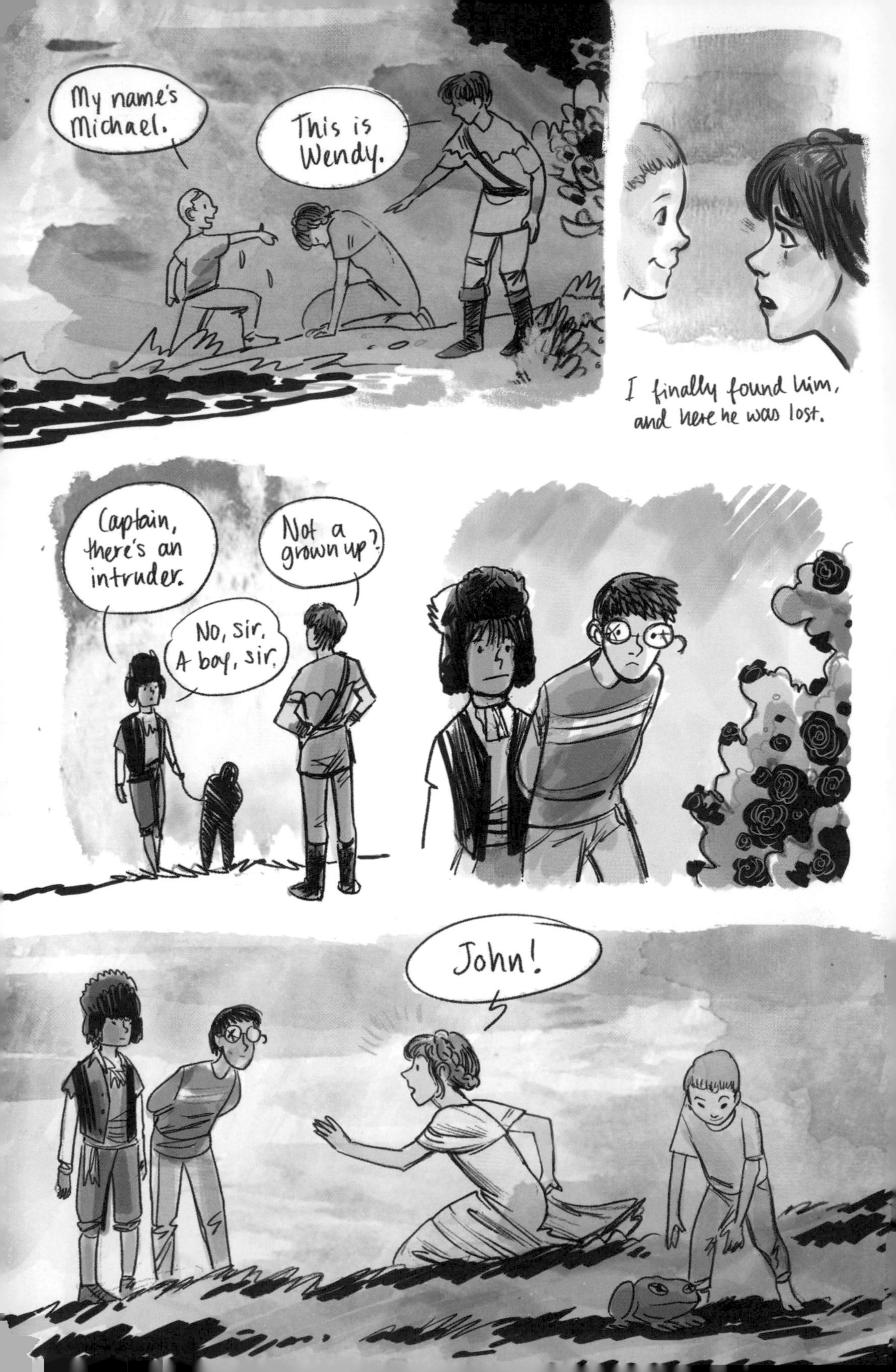

My name's Michael.
This is Wendy.
I finally found him, and here he was lost.
Captain, there's an intruder.
Not a grown up?
No, sir. A boy, sir.
John!

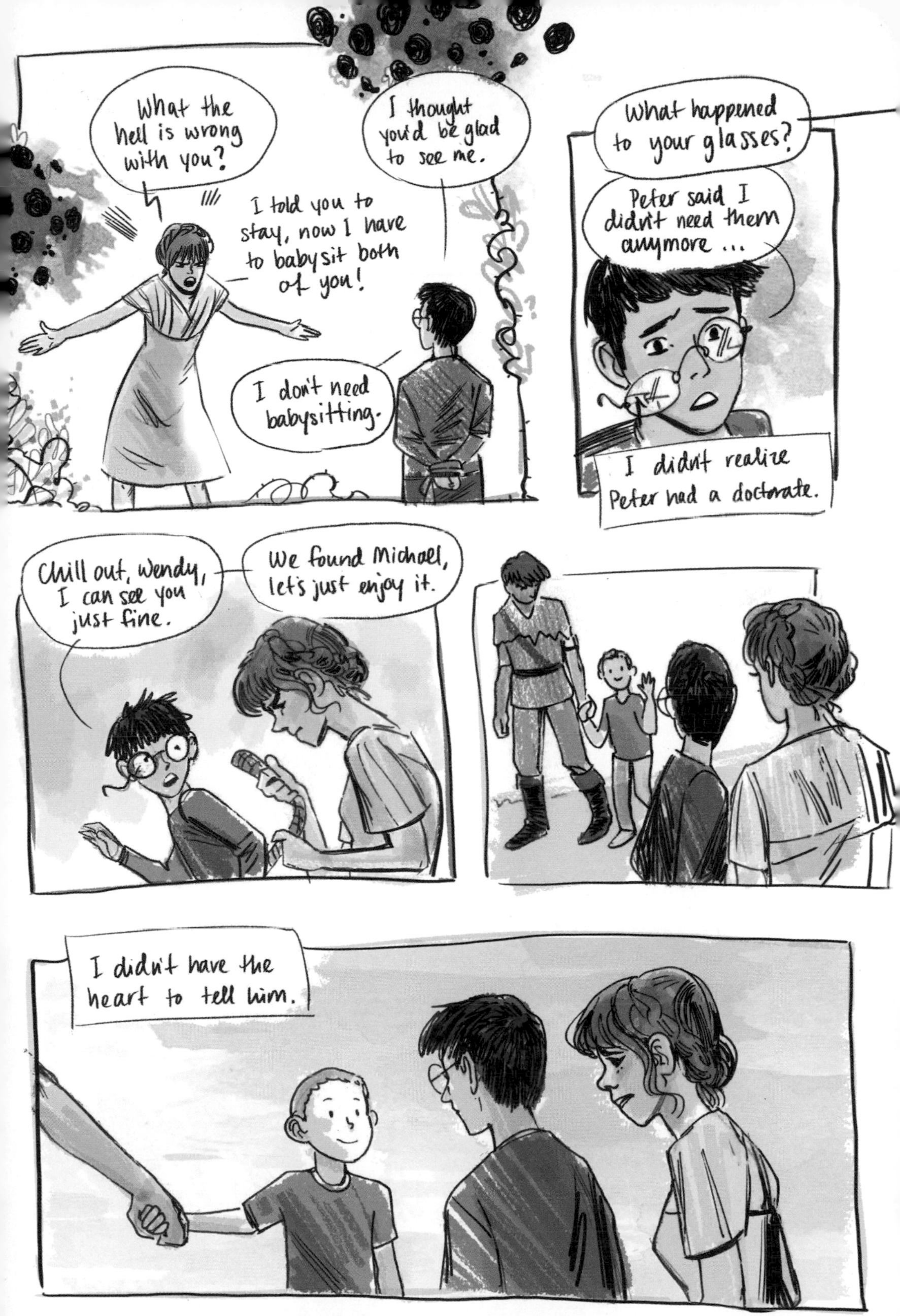
What the hell is wrong with you?
I told you to stay, now I have to babysit both of you!
I thought you'd be glad to see me.
I don't need babysitting.
What happened to your glasses?
Peter said I didn't need them anymore ...
I didn't realize Peter had a doctorate.
Chill out, Wendy, I can see you just fine.
We found Michael, let's just enjoy it.
I didn't have the heart to tell him.

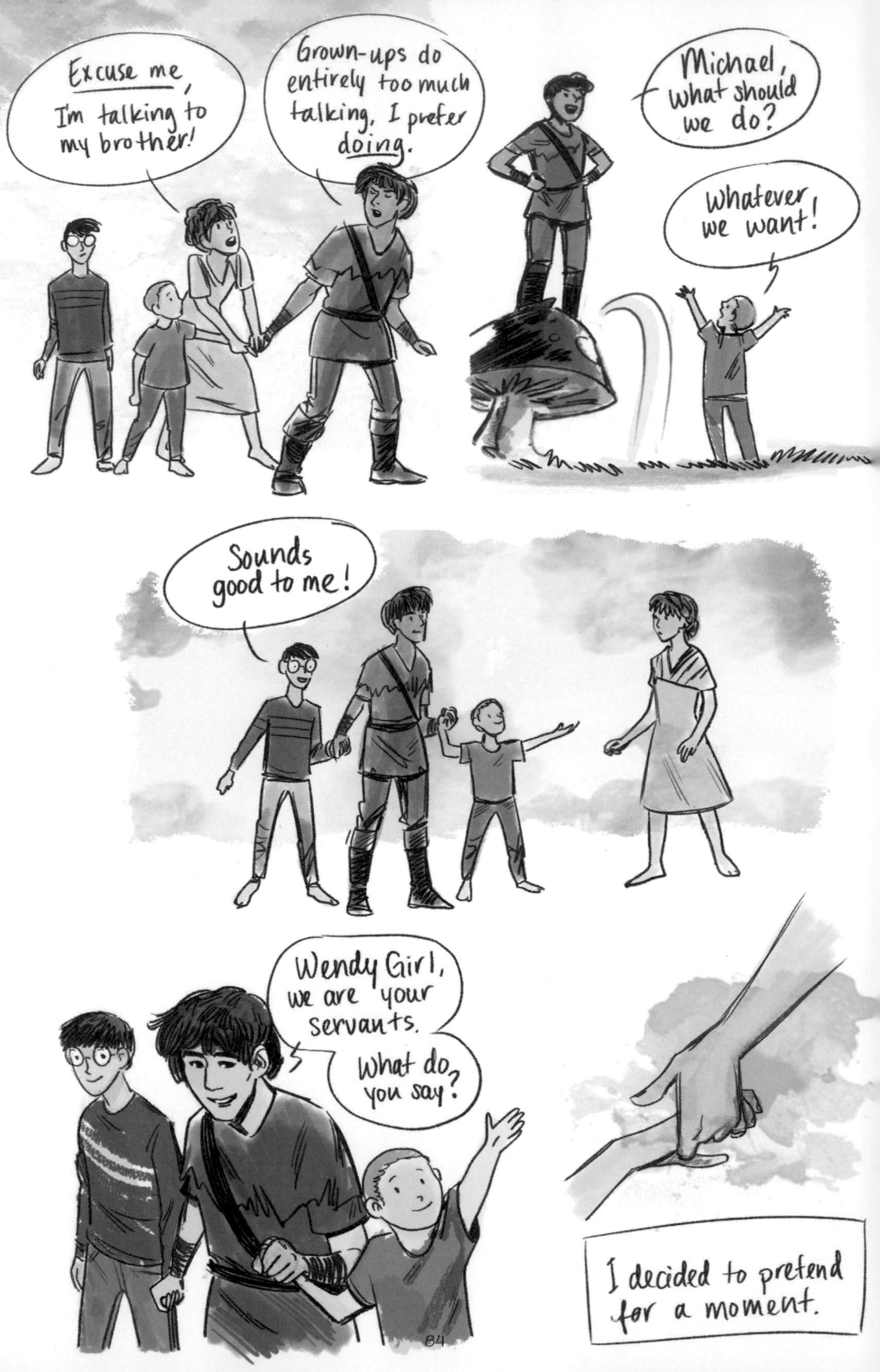
Excuse me, I'm talking to my brother!
Grown-ups do entirely too much talking. I prefer doing.
Michael, what should we do?
Whatever we want!
Sounds good to me!
Wendy Girl, we are your servants.
What do you say?
I decided to pretend for a moment.

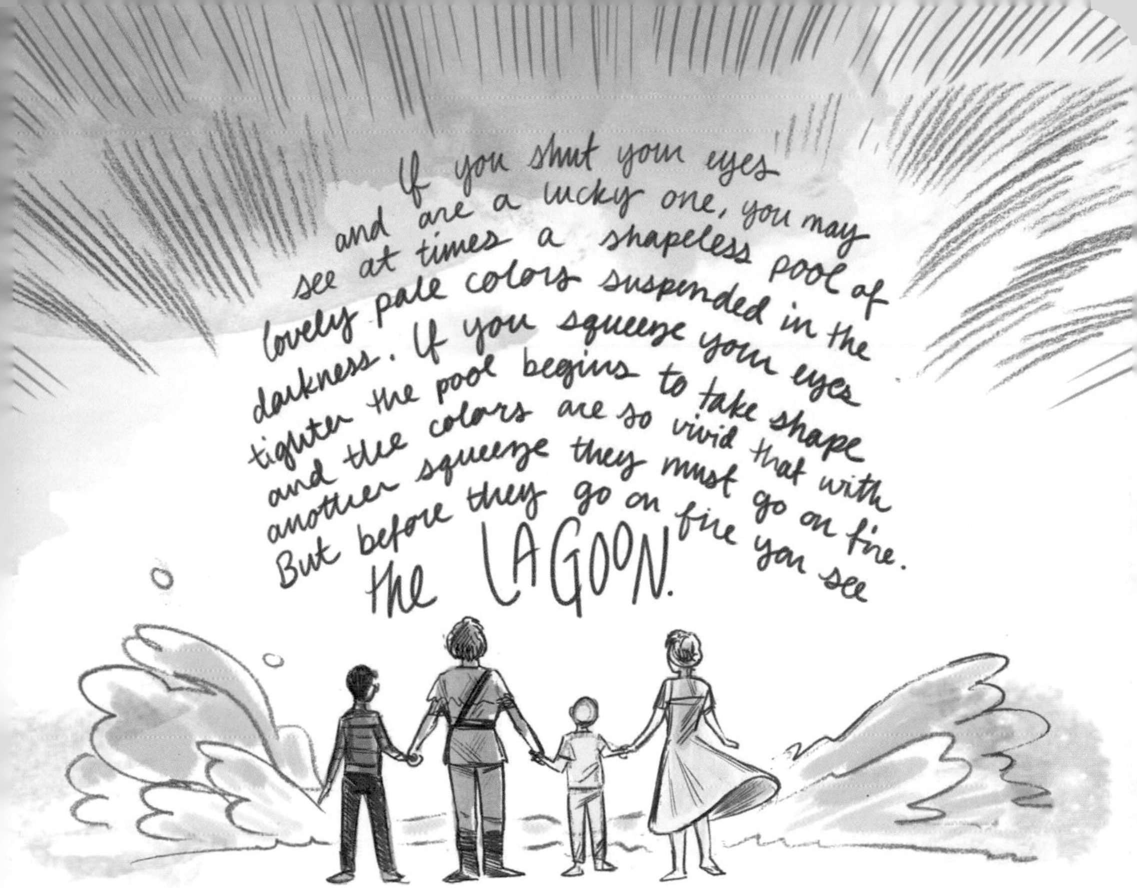
If you shut your eyes and are a lucky one, you may see at times a shapeless pool of lovely pale colors suspended in the darkness. If you squeeze your eyes tighter the pool begins to take shape and the colors are so vivid that with another squeeze they must go on fire. But before they go on fire you see THE LAGOON.

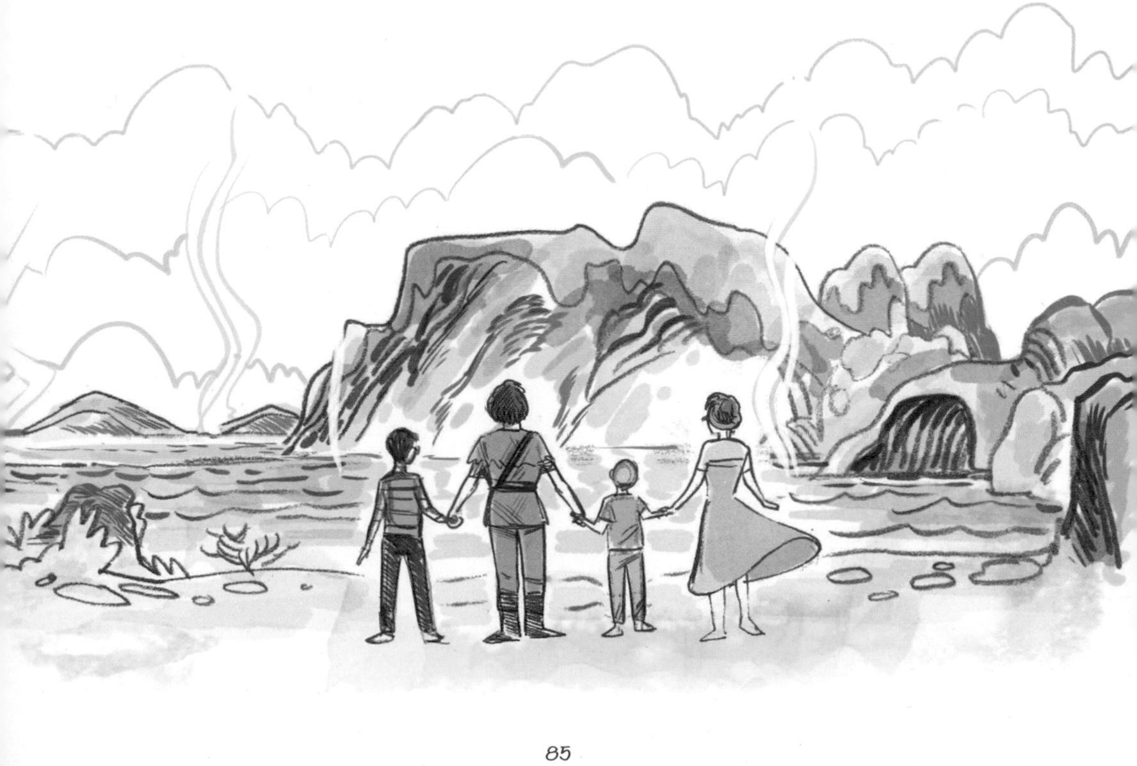

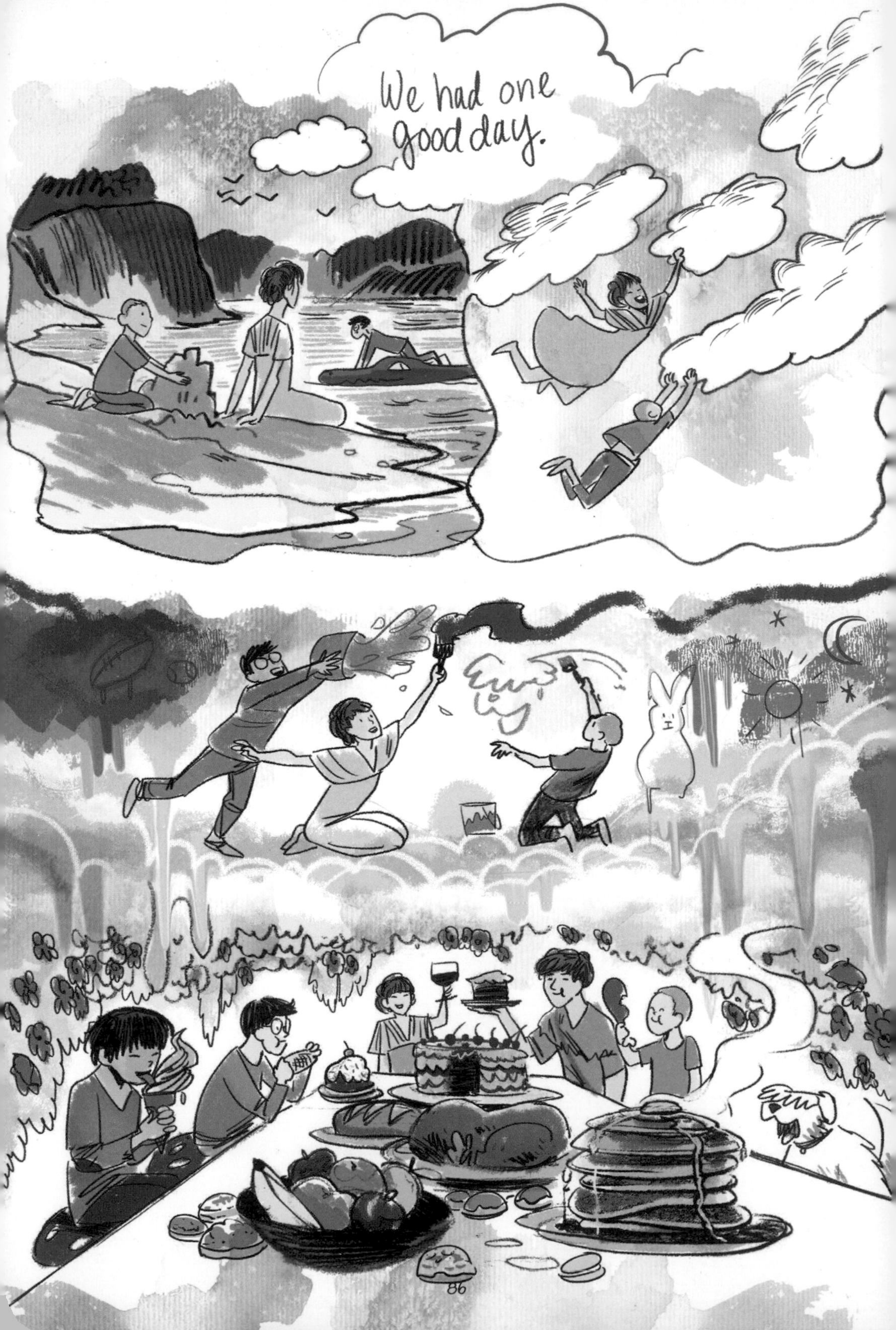
We had one good day.

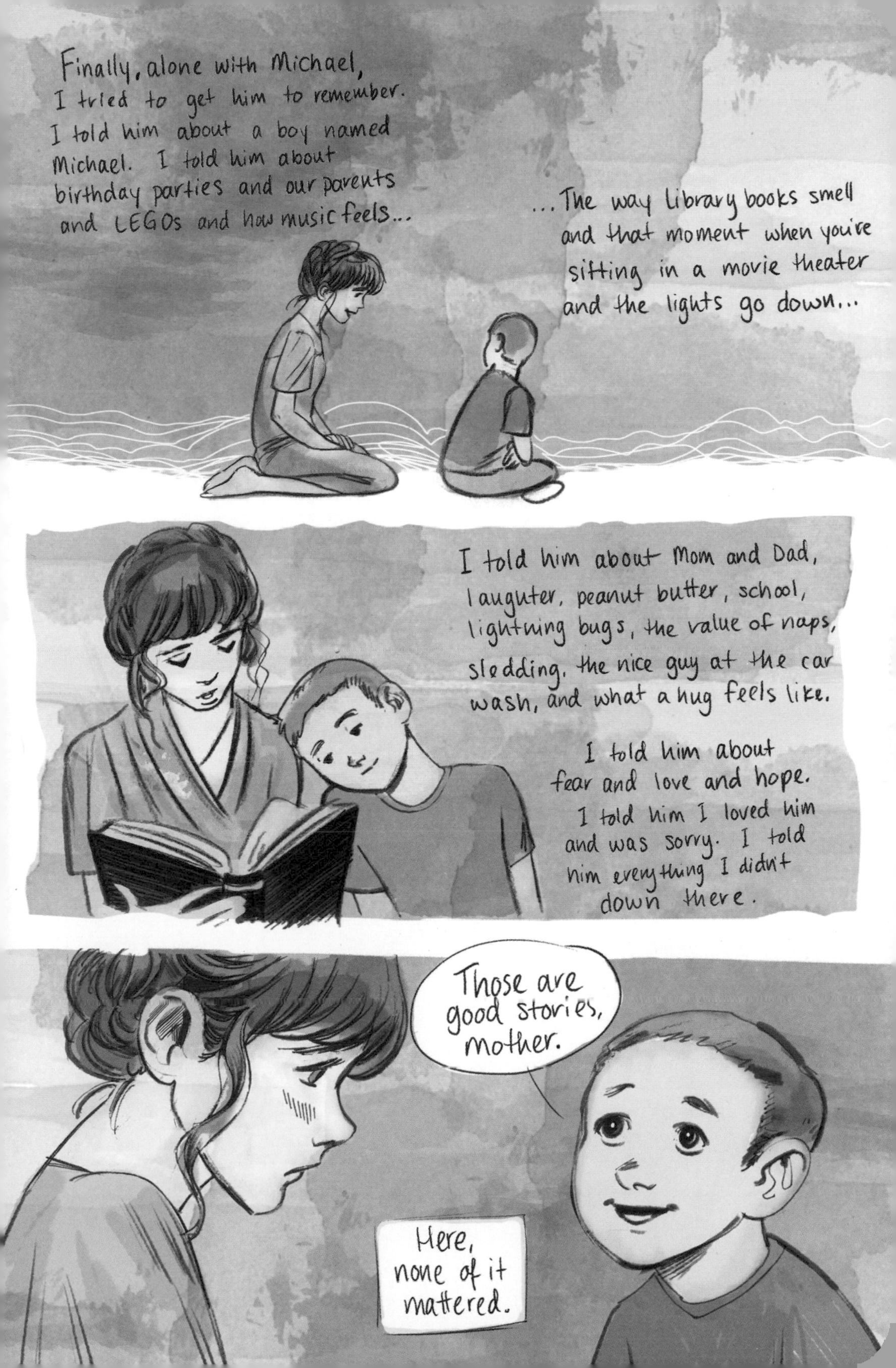
Finally, alone with Michael, I tried to get him to remember. I told him about a boy named Michael. I told him about birthday parties and our parents and LEGOs and how music feels...
...The way library books smell and that moment when you're sitting in a movie theater and the lights go down...
I told him about Mom and Dad, laughter, peanut butter, school, lightning bugs, the value of naps, sledding, the nice guy at the car wash, and what a hug feels like.
I told him about fear and love and hope. I told him I loved him and was sorry. I told him everything I didn't down there.
Those are good stories, mother.
Here, none of it mattered.

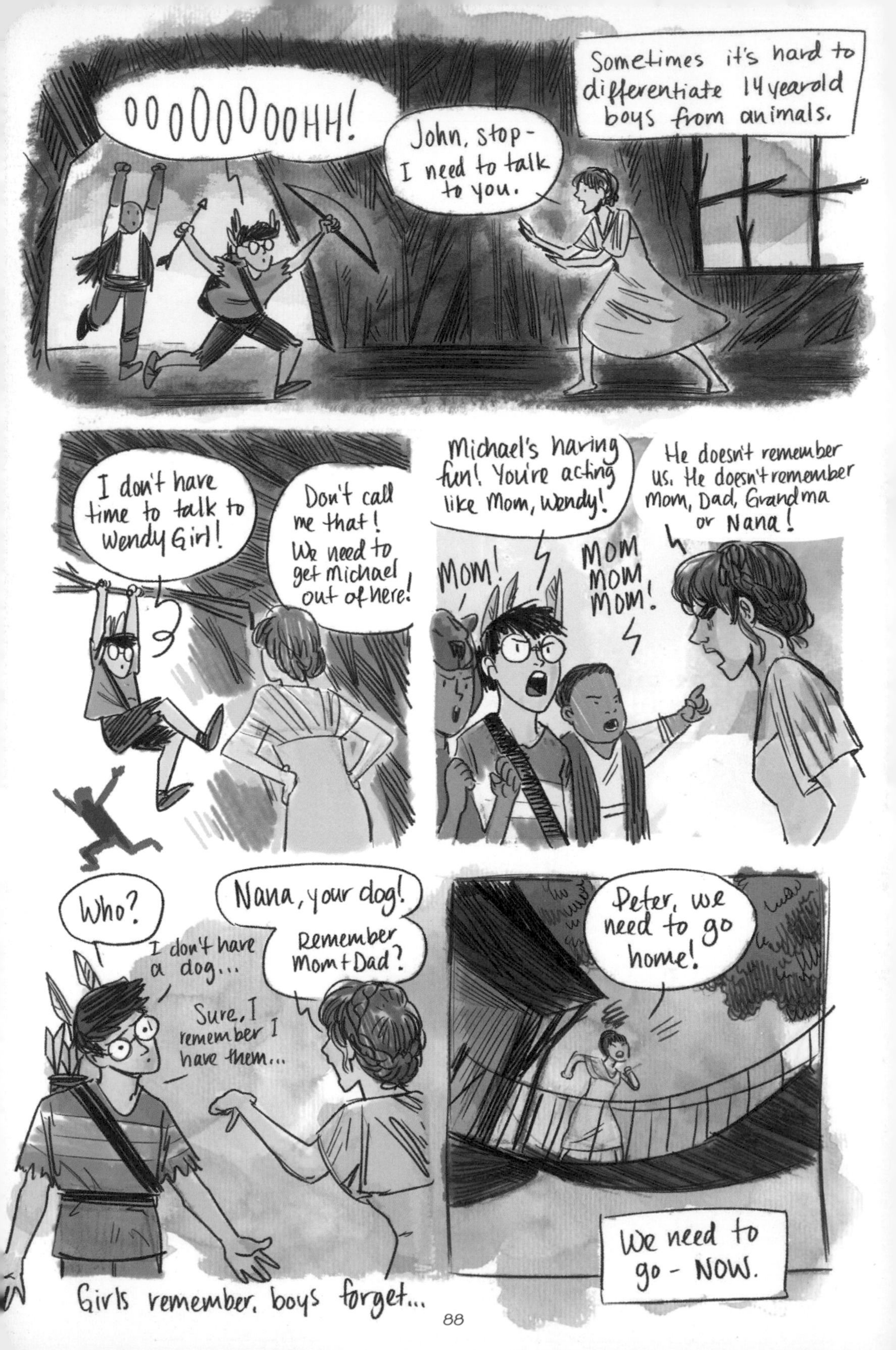
Sometimes it's hard to differentiate 14 yearold boys from animals.
OOOOOOOOHH!
John, stop - I need to talk to you.
I don't have time to talk to Wendy Girl!
Don't call me that! We need to get Michael out of here!
Michael's having fun! You're acting like Mom, Wendy!
MOM!
MOM MOM MOM!
He doesn't remember us. He doesn't remember Mom, Dad, Grandma or Nana!
Who?
I don't have a dog...
Nana, your dog!
Remember Mom+Dad?
Sure, I remember I have them...
Girls remember, boys forget...
Peter, we need to go home!
We need to go - NOW.

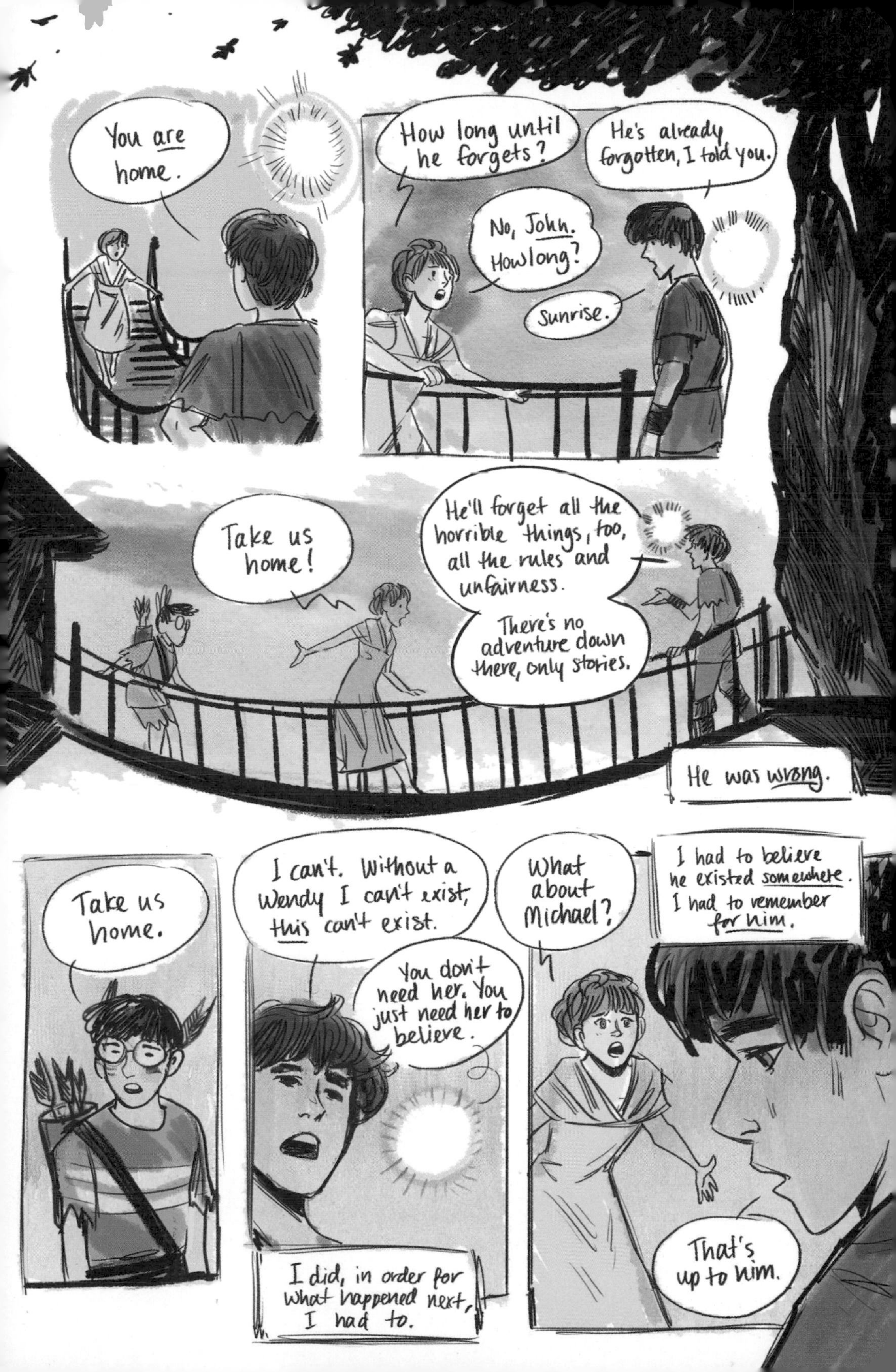
You are home.
How long until he forgets?
He's already forgotten, I told you.
No, John. How long?
Sunrise.
Take us home!
He'll forget all the horrible things, too, all the rules and unfairness.
There's no adventure down there, only stories.
He was wrong.
Take us home.
I can't. Without a Wendy I can't exist, this can't exist.
You don't need her. You just need her to believe.
I did, in order for what happened next, I had to.
What about Michael?
I had to believe he existed somewhere. I had to remember for him.
That's up to him.

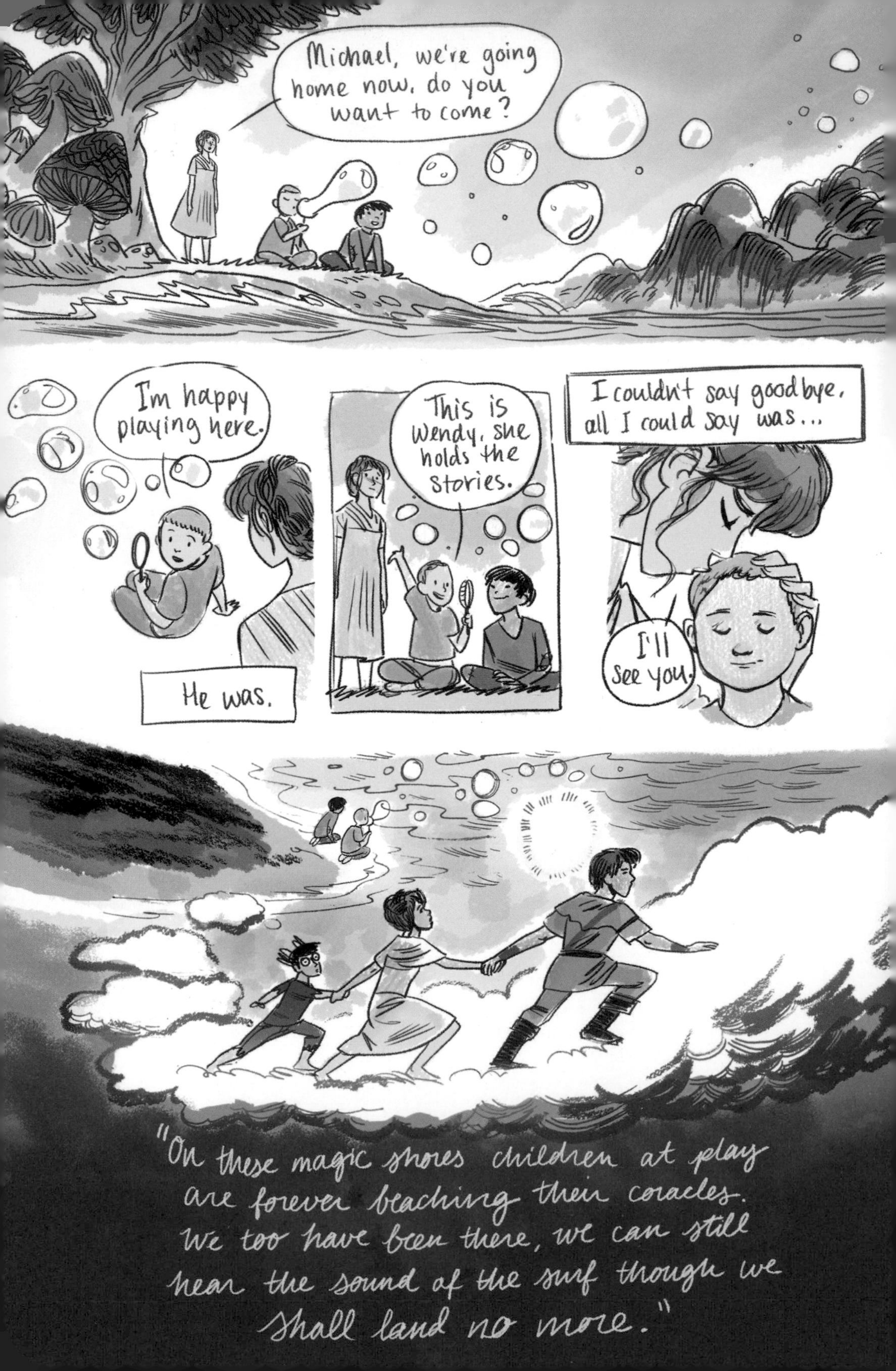
Michael, we're going home now. do you want to come?
I'm happy playing here.
He was.
This is Wendy, she holds the stories.
I couldn't say goodbye, all I could say was...
I'll see you.
"On these magic shores children at play are forever beaching their coracles. We too have been there, we can still hear the sound of the surf though we shall land no more."

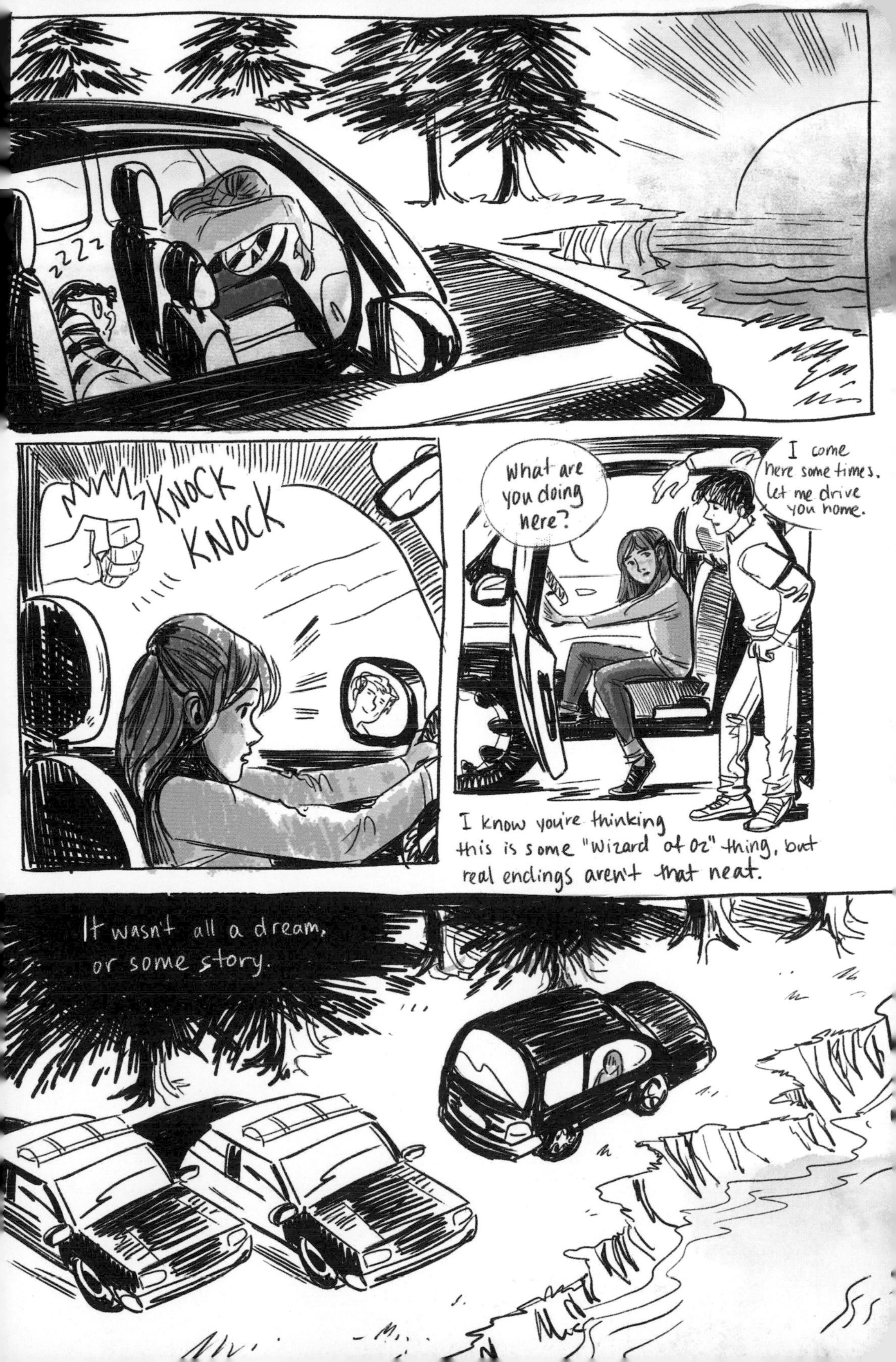

ZZZZ
KNOCK KNOCK
What are you doing here?
I come here some times. Let me drive you home.
I know you're thinking this is some "Wizard of Oz" thing, but real endings aren't that neat.
It wasn't all a dream, or some story.

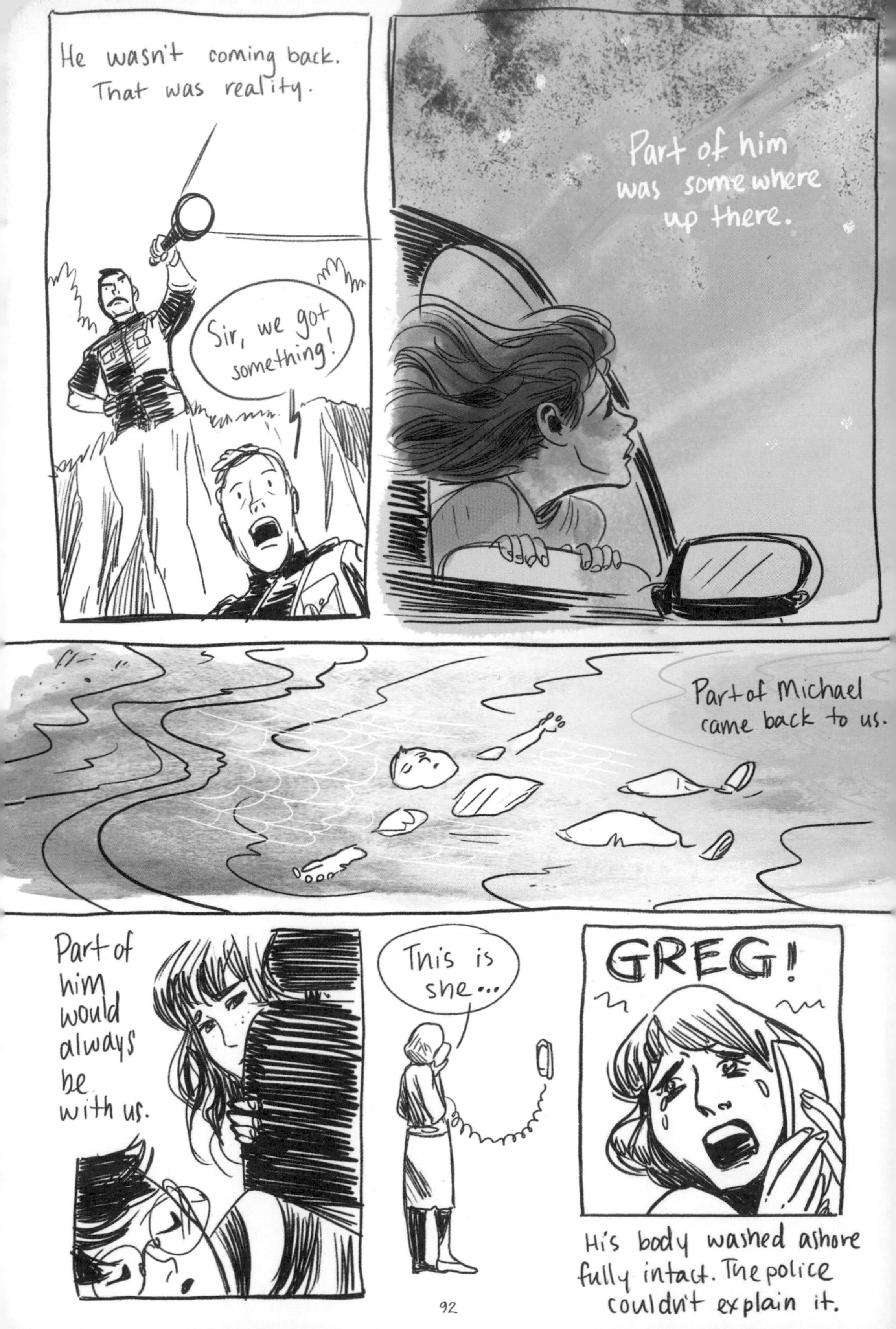
He wasn't coming back. That was reality.
Sir, we got something!
Part of him was somewhere up there.
Part of Michael came back to us.
Part of him would always be with us.
This is she...
GREG!
His body washed ashore fully intact. The police couldn't explain it.

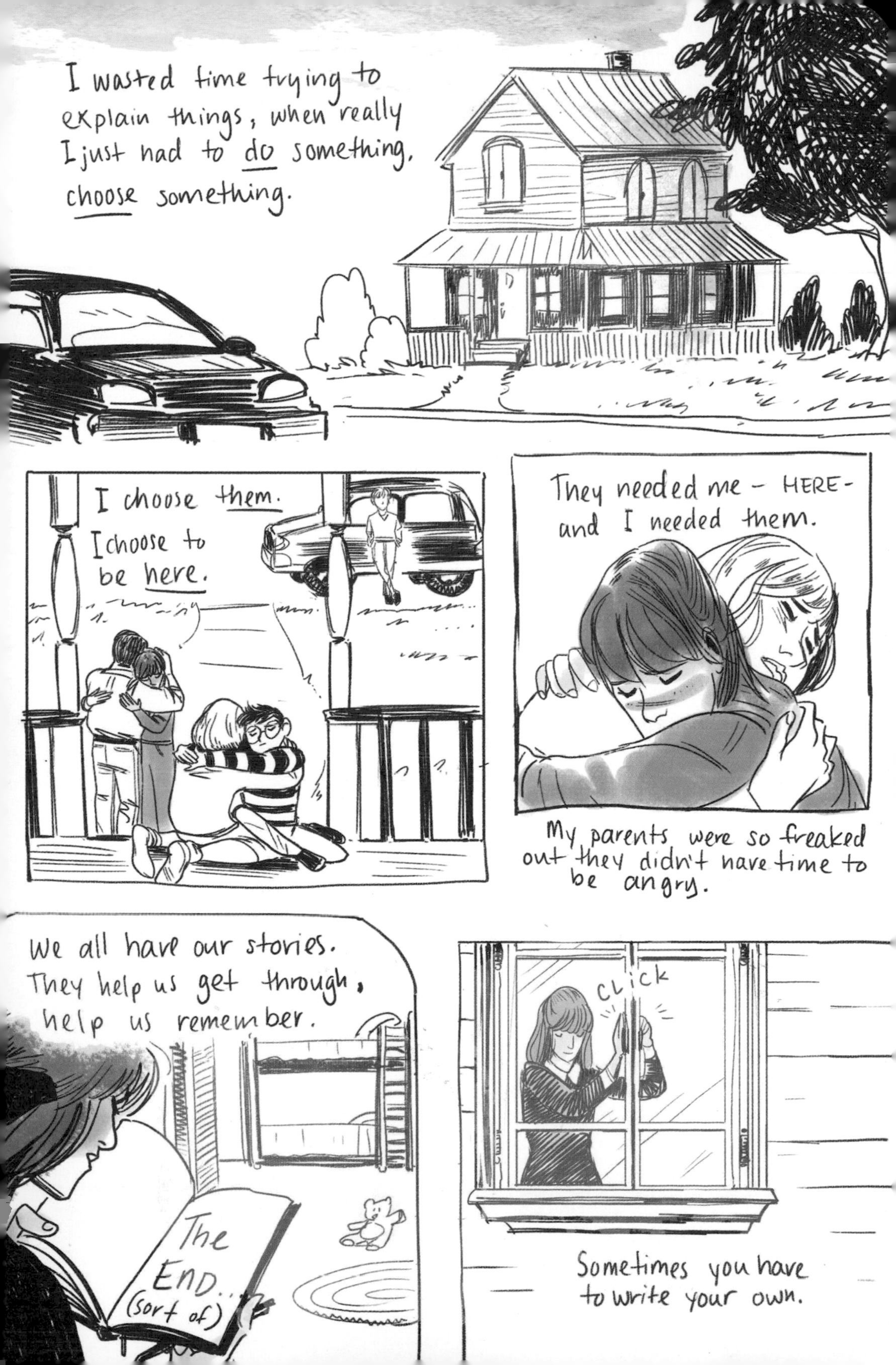
I wasted time trying to explain things, when really I just had to do something, choose something.
I choose them. I choose to be here.
They needed me - HERE - and I needed them.
My parents were so freaked out they didn't have time to be angry.
We all have our stories. They help us get through, help us remember.
The End... (sort of)
CLICK
Sometimes you have to write your own.

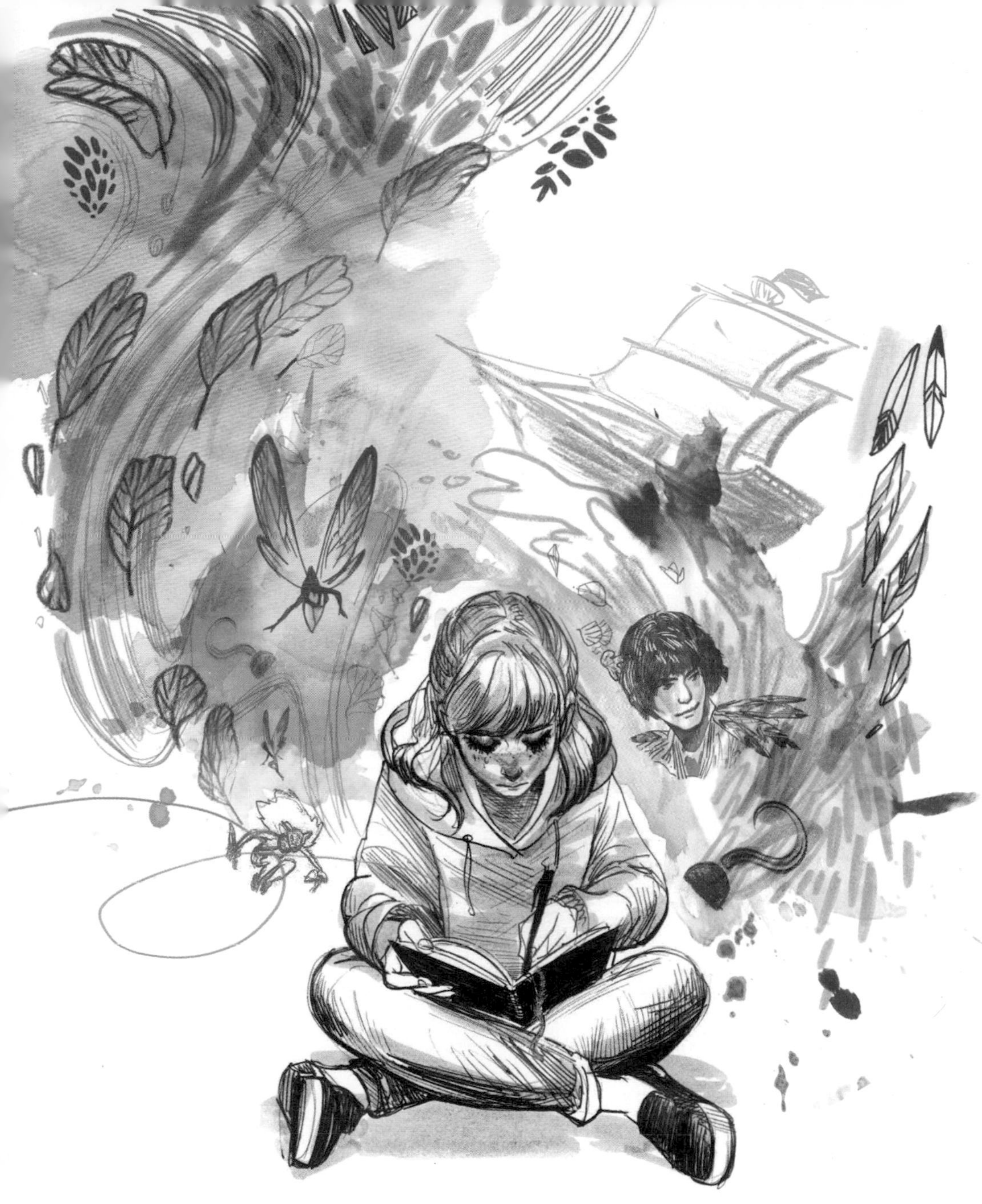

Melissa Jane Osborne is an actor and writer who has worked with Williamstown Theatre Festival, The Samuel French Festival, NYFringe, Killer Films, IAMA Theatre Co and Stella Adler Studio, of which she is an alum. She is a two time O'Neill National Playwrights Center finalist. Her work in new media spans from writing in various publications, to creating the first interactive scripted iPhone game "Campus Crush" for the Episode App. Her short film "Oma" starring Lynn Cohen is currently out to festivals nation wide. She is a proud member of LA's IAMA Theatre Co.

Veronica Fish has created illustrations for clients such as Nickelodeon, MARVEL, Wired Magazine, LEGO, The Girl Scouts of America and Conde Nast Publishing. Her paintings have been shown in galleries around the world, and she has drawn issues of Archie for Archie Comics, Spider-Woman and Silk for Marvel and is working on the next installment of her graphic novel Pirates of Mars with JJ Kahrs.

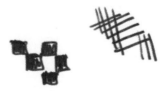